Better Living Through Laughter

An Attitude to Live By

STEPHEN PATTERSON

iUniverse, Inc.
New York   Bloomington

iUniverse books may be ordered through booksellers or by contacting:

iUniverse
1663 Liberty Drive
Bloomington, IN 47403
www.iuniverse.com
1-800-Authors (1-800-288-4677)

Because of the dynamic nature of the Internet, any Web addresses or links contained in this book may have changed since publication and may no longer be valid. The views expressed in this work are solely those of the author and do not necessarily reflect the views of the publisher, and the publisher hereby disclaims any responsibility for them.

ISBN: 978-1-4401-8922-7 (sc)
ISBN: 978-1-4401-8923-4 (ebook)

Printed in the United States of America

iUniverse rev. date: 12/21/09

Laughter:
the Gift that Keeps on Giving

Forward....

Everyone enjoys laughter. It is amazing how each person has their own special laugh. Is laughter learned? Is it taught in school? Is it genetic? It seems the answer to these questions is qualified. Laughter is something we are surrounded by but something we have to decide to use and benefit from.

Laughter is important to the entire civilized world. Everyone does it. We appreciate folks better if they have a sense of humor or will laugh with colleagues.

But… as important as laughter is in business, politics, religion, education, entertainment, military (maybe not here) and sex…. there is not a curriculum out there to teach folks how to laugh. We expect this most important human value to just happen…. On its own… magically and if not, there is a problem.

Just how valuable is laughter or humor?

Just think about the friends and family members who make you feel good. They are usually smiling, laughing and are just fun to be around. They are sharing stories about growing up, school, other friends and significant others. Usually the stories are fun to listen to as they recall happy events and activities. These stories help put us all in a better mood and help us feel better as well.

Steve Patterson is the kind- of- guy folks like to have around. If you ever meet him you would describe him as "likeable." In general conversation, he usually begins a sentence with a laugh, giving the signal that a positive moment is about to occur. He has a great memory of fun stories about your relationship with him and others. This is the kind of person you want around.

Just like Garrison Keillor of Prairie Home Companion fame, Steve has stories about his hometown of Sanford, NC and his college years at Elon College. His humorous stories would lead one to believe he grew up and was educated on the Andy Griffin show.

The memories of his school chums, teachers, favorite hangouts, sports and especially his dates, fictitious or not, are part of his makeup. We have heard about Sanford so many times that we feel we have grown up there. His best friends are our friends. The power of his humor is reflected in his friendships and relationships. For Steve laughter is a fuel for a positive life.

I have known Steve for a little over thirty years and have never grown tired of his humor, stories and laughter. His sense of humor is contagious all of the folks around him seem to like his company. I have witnessed his children grow up. They too are positive exhibiting some of the same good traits that Steve lives by. Which leads me to believe attitudes may not be genetic but it can be learned.

I feel that everyone is born with an ability to laugh. Some of us are maybe even predisposed to have a better sense of humor. But we all should foster the growth of our sense of humor. It needs to be nurtured and exercised regularly.

Listen and learn from your inner voice and you will begin begin to realize laughing is a great part of living the good life. Steve Patterson has learned this and has spent much of his life as a model for his friends and colleagues… a model of how to get along with others in a complex and competitive world. We should listen to the words of Steve in this book and really learn how to daily commit to **Better Living Through Laughter!**

Bob Noe
Carolina Learning Solutions

Acknowledgements

There are numerous people who should be singled out for their support. Many of whom I never knew their name. But they participated and listened to my presentations and workshops on the value of humor. Their laughter and support indicated I indeed had something worthwhile to share. I especially want to thank my family. They have supplied me with countless hours of love, encouragement and laughter. Over the years my family has proven to be one of my greatest resources of humor. Every day my family makes me smile and gives me joy. So to my family, my audiences—both old and new—and everyone with whom I have shared a laugh or enjoyed a smile I say thank you.

Introduction

Outside the door leading to my parents' back deck, I heard what can only be described as a small-scale ruckus. Approaching the door the noise grew louder. The sound of an animal in distress rang out. Pulling back the floor length drapes I spotted the source of the noise: my oversized, yellow and white cat, PC (Privileged Character). PC was attempting to bring his latest catch into the house. PC seemed to feel the need to share his conquests with everyone and this night was no different as he stood at the door holding a large gray rabbit in his mouth.

If I was going to save the rabbit I needed to move quickly. In the same motion as I opened the door I bent down and slapped the cat causing him to release the rabbit. Unfortunately for the rabbit his misfortunes were not over. Once freed from the jaws of death he immediately jumped to what he may have assumed was freedom. On this night freedom was going to come at a price. His leap carried him off the 10-foot deck. As he sailed off the deck you would have thought his problems were over. And maybe they would have been if he had actually hit the ground. No, he fell 10 feet into a five-gallon bucket of rain water. Talk about your bad days. I was able to free him from the bucket a little shaken but he seemed fine as he hopped away. PC on the other hand was a little upset that he had lost his catch, but seemed to be fine as well. The entire incident took only a few seconds but it has supplied much more laughter over the years. It was one of *America's Funniest Videos* long before there was such a show.

Why do I remember this story so well? Not for some humanitarian reason. I remember it because it was funny. For over 30 years I have shared this tale with others and it still brings about smiles and chuckles. This is the power of a good laugh. Laughter can be a link to childhood memories, embarrassing situations or friendly conversations. This is a prime example of how humor can be found in all areas of life and, in many times, when we least expect it.

Laughter is defined as the manifestation of joy or mirth. That's the clinical definition. Of course, a simpler definition would be the ability to express joy in a physical manner. Maybe this too is a little too clinical. It would be less clinical to say laughter is a physical display of positive feelings and emotions. Everyone seems to enjoy laughter, and why not? The benefits of a good laugh last long after the physical act has passed. Most likely your favorite memories are the ones that include a good dose of laughter. Laughter knows no boundaries and may breakout at anytime and can be freely shared by everyone. Laughter also knows no social or economic barrier. Everyone can enjoy it.

From work to play laughter should be present. Hopefully you have enjoyed laughter in all areas of your life. Maybe you experience it daily in the home sharing a joke or a story with a loved one or possibly when you watch children at play. At work humor and laughter can make the five o'clock grind turn into the five o'clock grin. The true magic of laughter is how available it is to everyone. Laughter has no age barrier old and young alike, can enjoy it. The only barriers to humor are the ones we place on it.

Everyone is born with the ability to enjoy laughter. You can't put a price tag on laughter—it's free to everyone. The availability of laughter is abundant and it is as essential as oxygen, food or love. Laughter has many wonderful side effects helping us physically and mentally. Laughter is a universal language and can be enjoyed and understood by everyone.

I have always felt laughter is a wonderful emotion because it is unique to the individual, yet it can be shared and enjoyed by everyone. We may not appreciate the same types of humor but if we are sharing a laugh then we are making a positive connection. When a connection is forged with laughter, good things happen.

Laughter has always been an important part of my life. As a child I enjoyed the humor my family shared. The positive affects of laughter helped me appreciate the good times more and enabled me to make it through some tough and tragic times as well. I still cherish laughter and I continue to share it with my family and friends. The laughter we share helps make every day more enjoyable. I have recognized the benefits of enjoying laughter in all aspects of my life. When it comes to sharing laughter there is nothing better. The sheer enjoyment delivered from a laugh is hard to match or duplicate.

The old saying, "A day without laughter is like a day without sunshine," probably has more truth than we realize. If we are not laughing or enjoying laughter we are missing out on a wonderful emotion—an emotion that separates man from animals. The ability to enjoy laughter and use humor is one of the best traits of mankind, with countless benefits.

Too often laughter is taken for granted. If we begin taking laughter for granted we will begin to lose sight of its importance. Though laughter is free and bountiful we should never lose sight of its importance. Laughter can be a fuel for a good life.

Though I have always enjoyed laughter and it has always been part of my life I never really considered the value of a laugh, until I began to study laughter. While studying laughter I soon realized how it positively affected my life. I learned that laughter affects everything I do whether it's social or professional. Laughter has been, and remains, a vital ingredient to my personal growth and survival.

If you go through life and fail to enjoy laughter you will cheat yourself out of a great resource for a healthy life. Take a moment to think about your personal laughter and what it means to you. What role does humor play in your everyday life? Do you look for humor? Do you share laughter? All of these questions and more will be asked, and hopefully answered, in the following chapters. Hopefully we will begin to understand laughter and the role it plays in our life as we learn **Better Living through Laughter.**

Chapter 1

Born to Laugh

It has been said that it's important to know where you come from as you chart your course for where you are going. If this is the case, then it is easy to see why laughter is so important in my life. Laughter helps identify who I am. In school, I may not have been the class clown, but I certainly knew who was. Laughter has always been present in my life—in school, in my home, at work and in my community. Once I began the study of humor it didn't take long to recognize the important role laughter has played in my life. My favorite memories are filled with laughter. My studies gave me the idea to begin the development of workshops and presentations that focused on the value of humor and a good laugh.

Originally my hope was to show others how something as simple as a good laugh could pay dividends on our physical and mental health. As I developed these workshops and presentations I soon assumed the role of a pied piper of humor. I have been singing the praises of laughter ever since. (Okay, not really singing, but you get my point.)

The workshops and presentation are designed to help each participant learn the value of his or her sense of humor—hopefully learning how a good laugh can make a bad day better and a good day great. I also developed a humor partnership with co-worker and fellow trainer Bob Noe. Bob and I share a love of laughter that led us to work together.

Bob and I have worked together on various projects for over 25 years and the one constant in our friendship and our professional relationship has been the sharing of laughter. In our workshops, we introduce participants to the many physical and mental advantages of laughter and how self-confidence and self-esteem are enhanced with a good laugh. We try to demonstrate how a good laugh can give us needed strength when facing many of life's greatest challenges. Presenting these workshops has grown into a labor of love that we both enjoy thoroughly. In truth, we would probably give the presentations to anyone who would listen. For me, presenting humor workshops gives me the opportunity to share laughter with others. It's hard to put a price on that. The joy of a shared laugh is priceless.

In high school I discovered that humor helped me fit in and get along with classmates and teachers. I learned that a smile would carry me further than a frown. It was also in high school that I had my first taste of comedic performance. Though I may not have been known as the class clown, I developed a reputation for some of my attempts at humor. I often clowned around with my friends by doing routines and telling jokes—all in an effort to produce a laugh. During these years I tried my hand at impersonations. I became known for my "John Wayne" and "Jimmy Stewart" and a few others. My friends have always known of my passion for humor and how much I enjoy creating and sharing laughter. Many of them consider me a frustrated comedian. If I was frustrated, it was a result of my lack of talent. But the lack of talent has never diminished my love for comedy and a good laugh.

In high school I got an opportunity to do some stand-up comedy and it was a highlight of my senior year. My big break, or what I thought was a big break, came at an end-of-the-year school dance. At the dance my friends encouraged and dared me to do some comedy. When the band took a break I took the stage. I proceeded to do an impromptu stand-up routine. Up until that night my impersonations were done for small groups, mostly limited to friends. On this night that all changed. Though my classmates did offer up a friendly crowd, it was a crowd just the same. I copied the great impressionists of the era, Rich Little and Frank Gorshin. In reality, what people were getting were my impersonations of impersonators doing impersonations. But on this night it was not Gorshin or Little. It was Steve Patterson. I was doing the impersonations and enjoying the moment. I was excited and thrilled trying my hand at entertaining the crowd at Sanford Central High—a crowd that had meant so much to me over the years.

Like with most school dances, our cafeteria had been decorated to resemble a fine hotel and we had a local garage band supplying the music. I don't remember the name of the band or even if they were any good. All I remember from that night was taking the stage and the laughter from my classmates; it remains one of my favorite memories. Fortunately everyone was having a great time—excitement about the end of the school year and our approaching graduation had everyone in a good mood. So, even the worst critic couldn't help enjoy that night. And a little stand-up comedy from a rank amateur wasn't going to spoil the evening. I was thrilled to share my routines.

I had a very attentive audience and my efforts to entertain were well received. I'm sure no one else remembers that night, but I sure do. I can recall the night with little effort remembering the good feeling all the while smiling to myself. My impersonations included a look at life in high school as seen through the eyes of the greats of the day—people like John Wayne, Kurt Douglas and Jimmy Stewart. But my best impersonation was of my high school tennis coach, Charles Alexander. The biggest laughs came at his expense. Coach Alexander was a fine man who knew little about tennis and drew the shortest straw when he got the assignment to coach the sport. Unfortunately, his lack of knowledge led him to become the butt of a lot of jokes—none of which were deserved. He had a distinctive accent that was easily duplicated. Everyone could identify Coach Alexander. I tried to show the class how Coach Alexander would handle John Wayne trying out for the tennis team or how Jimmy Stewart would have introduced him to his doubles partner: a 6-foot-3-inch white rabbit named Harvey. The evening was full of laughter. I truly enjoyed my 15 minutes of fame and I still do years later.

My reality check bounced.

No doubt that this experience was a springboard to my desire to share laughter with others. I learned that there is nothing quite as contagious as laughter and if you are the instigator it provides quite a rush. Little did I know at the time that making people laugh would become a goal that would stay with me through the years. It would be some time before I would take the public stage again. Though I continued to do my impersonations; my efforts were generally limited to small gatherings or parties. Still, I maintained the desire to share and instigate laughter.

Reflecting on my use of humor I am aware that there were times that my humor may not have been appreciated as much as I had hoped. An example of this was on my first job out of college. The desire to use humor landed me in a little hot water. I was in a management training program for a national clothing retailer. Fortunately it didn't take me long to realize that my future did not lie in retail. Shortly after giving my two-week notice the temptation to have a little fun overtook me. While sitting at my desk in the back of the store I used the intercom system to broadcast the following announcement.

"Pat would you bring me a cheeseburger, hamburger, lettuce and tomato, French fry corn pone and a hash-brown potato?"

This rhythmical request was heard throughout the store. Who knows, it could have been the first rap song in Winston Salem. Maybe I should have recorded it. Anyway, it didn't take long for the manager to appear at my door angrily requesting that we keep it professional, as he attempted to hold back his laughter.

Not long after I left the company and gave up my attempt at retail management, the chain went bankrupt and later out of business. Maybe if the corporation would have allowed for a little more humor they would still be in business…

The roots of my humor can definitely be traced back to my childhood. Most behavior patterns demonstrated as adults are rooted in childhood influences. Bob and I not only share an active sense of humor but we were also raised in military families; our fathers had long careers in the Air Force. Military brats are afforded many experiences—some good, some not so good, but experiences just the same. When you grow up as a military brat you usually experience living in various parts of the world or country, coming in contact with diverse cultures and individuals. Bob and I both enjoyed our experiences as military brats and we were lucky enough to have experiences that we may not have been exposed to if not for the many moves our families made.

Everyone in the family was affected when father's orders changed. The moves produced a fair amount of stress, but the moves also produced some fun and excitement. An outgrowth of these many moves was the bond our family developed.

When Bob and I compared stories about growing up on an Air Force base we realized both our families enjoyed a great deal of laughter no matter where we lived. Both of us share the belief that laughter helped define our families. It also helped lay the foundation for the way we approach life today.

When my father retired from the Air Force we settled in central North Carolina close to my parents' original home. Though our travels had lessened the humor bond continued. I will always cherish the memories of how my parents used their sense of humor daily.

Families that share laughter typically have a greater appreciation for each other and they understand the need for a loving, supportive environment. Families are more likely to share their love and support when laughter is present. To this day, my brother Barry and I still enjoy a special relationship—

one that grew out of cross country trips full of laughter and adventure.

These cross country trips tested our creative nature as we searched for ways to pass time and entertain ourselves. We enjoyed telling stories and playing games. One of my favorite activities was holding a laughing contest between the two of us. The object of the game was to see who could make the other laugh first and most. Unfortunately, being the youngest in the family, I found almost everything he did to be funny. He, on the other hand, practiced great restraint and self-control and would hardly crack a smile at my lame attempts at humor. Seldom did I muster a laugh or a chuckle from him. This may be the underlying reason I started doing humor workshops: I'm still trying to win a laughing contest.

In the years prior to in-car DVD players or iPods, Barry and I knew if we were going to have entertainment we would have to create it. Long car rides only magnified this need. The interstate highway system was in its infancy, so most of our travels were confined to the back roads of America. These back road adventures provided me with many a memory. Thankfully no matter where or when we traveled our family enjoyed laughter. Laughter was a tool we used to fight off boredom and anxiety. Necessity maybe the mother of invention but in our household anxiety and boredom proved to be the mother of humor.

During these trips it seemed our parents took on certain responsibilities or roles. My father was a gifted storyteller. He entertained us with stories of his youth and childhood. Many of his tales live on today as I have passed them on to my children, knowing that there is no statute of limitations for funny. Family stories help keep the memories alive—a wonderful tribute to family and friends that may have lived years ago.

Dad grew up on a tobacco farm in rural North Carolina. He loved to describe his large family as having "eight boys all of whom had two sisters." For a brief second people would have to think twice about the size of his family. Raised during the Great Depression, he certainly needed a good sense of humor. Not only did he have a need for a good sense of humor, he needed to use it daily. His family possessed little more than each other; so they relied on their own efforts and initiatives for amusement and survival. Dad would entertain us for hours talking about his life on the farm. He gave us a humorous take on all his brothers and sisters and, with such a large family, you can bet there was a lot of humor. Though we lived in different communities and saw our aunts and uncles only once a year, these stories gave Barry and I a chance to get to know our aunts and uncles in a unique fashion. We were able to learn what our father's siblings were really like and understand the amount of love he had for his family.

One of my favorite stories of my father's was a tale about a great baseball game between his family and a group of cousins. The game turned out to be a marathon game that lasted well into the evening on a hot August day. The game lasted so long they were forced to hang lanterns to light the contest's finish. Daddy claimed this resulted in the first night game ever played in Harnett County. The game was a classic pitcher's duo that lasted 36 innings. My father claimed he pitched the entire game with his arm becoming so heated that between innings he had to submerge it in a bucket of ice water just to keep it cool. On the opposing mound was his cousin George. George also pitched the entire game but his efforts left him a little worse for the wear. It seems the punishment on his pitching hand resulted in his fingers being worn down to the knuckles. The whole story of overheated arms and worn down knuckles created a vision that made everyone laugh. Every time Barry or I would be called on to pitch in our youth baseball days we heard this story. Maybe he felt the story would inspire us to try our hardest when playing ball. Or, it was his way of trying to relax us—allowing us to see the fun in playing ball. No matter his reasoning, I never wanted to pitch to the point my fingers wore down to my knuckles or, for that matter, have the need to dip my arm in a bucket of ice water.

Though I always appreciated this story it wasn't until years later that it really made me laugh. While attending a family reunion I met Cousin George and, to my shock, the fingers on his right hand were indeed cut off at the knuckles. Now, I still don't believe cousin George's short fingers were the result of his pitching in an extended game but it did create some laughter. When I recount many of my father's stories I can see how he would take real life situations, embellish them a little, add some humor and come up with quite a tale that entertained everyone.

Daddy also shared stories about his brother Gilbert who may have been a taco shy of a combination plate. Daddy felt that Gilbert didn't *suffer* from mental illness but rather, he *enjoyed* it. Daddy told us that Gilbert tried various occupations. One of which was raising chickens. But this venture was met with little success. Daddy said it was a failure because Gilbert either planted the chickens too close together or a little too deep. Gilbert was also an inventive type. One of his inventions was Spam on a rope for those who got hungry in the shower.

It should be noted that we did have an Uncle Gilbert but all of the stories my father told about him were the result of Daddy's active imagination. Gilbert just happens to be the brother that became the blunt of Daddy's jokes. This was how my father personalized his stories. Though we knew there was little truth in his tales we still found them to be very entertaining.

Gilbert was not the only one in the family that Daddy enjoyed telling stories about—he also amused us with tall tales of our great grandfather, Sherd Patterson. Sherd was the polar opposite of Gilbert. Sherd could do no wrong. He was actually capable of accomplishing feats of greatness. Daddy would bring to life the many adventures of Sherd Patterson. His tales made Sherd larger than life. His stories gave us the impression that he had mystic powers that he could use to change the world. From digging rivers to winning wars, you name it: Sherd accomplished it.

To this day, every time I cross the Cape Fear River in North Carolina I think how Daddy would tell us how Sherd had dug the river in his youth creating a direct route to the coast. Barry, on an explorer trip down the river, shared the story with his scout mates and master and he was told by his scout master that if Sherd did indeed dig the river, he must have been drinking some Cox whiskey because the river was so crooked! Everyone enjoyed the story and it added to the fun of the trip.

We came to believe that Sherd was the Patterson equivalent to Paul Bunyan. Almost every small town in the south has a center square with a statue honoring the men and women of past wars. It was not unusual for Daddy to claim these statues were indeed erected to honor Sherd. It seemed to make little difference what era the statue represented—it was always Sherd. Every time I see such a statue today I think of Daddy and the stories of my great-grandfather Sherd.

Sherd did have a colorful life. He fought in the Civil War and was shot in the chest. The bullet was never removed and eventually it led to his death some 20 later as it worked its way to his heart. Maybe his life wasn't as colorful as Daddy wanted everyone to believe, but he had his share of stories.

At 17, my father chose to leave his home and join the military where he went on to fight in two wars and serve his country honorably for over 30 years. Throughout his life, his sense of humor never left him. My mother used to tell us the story of how she and my Daddy met. Daddy was home on leave and while on a blind date he told my mother he would be home for 30 days and he wanted 30 dates. I'm not sure they had the 30 dates but they did have over 45 years of marriage—another indication of how Daddy's humor served him well.

As children, Barry and I not only enjoyed our father's sense of humor, but we also learned to appreciate his love for adventure. I don't know if it was a need for a break or his love for fun but he had the rare quality and patience to stop and visit almost every roadside attraction we happened by. In those days there were plenty of roadside adventures to visit. From Dog Patch in Tennessee to the gravity-defying cottage in Colorado—you name it, we stopped at it. We visited them all and it was great fun. To this day I have a pencil drawing of a barn with "Visit Rock City" on its roof as a reminder of these trips. Other kids went to Disneyland. We went to the hideout for Jesse James. These adventures helped us learn an appreciation for life and its humor. As a parent, I have even more appreciation for father's willingness to stop at these attractions—especially as I struggle with my need to get to the next destination rather than enjoying the trip. Too often I have driven on by and not given the roadside attraction a second thought. My father, by his stopping at these attractions, was in his own way stopping to smell the roses.

I believe both my parents had a special understanding of laughter and humor and it was always present. Barry and I were no different from other children—we got ourselves into plenty of trouble. But as I think back on those times and situations I can't help but smile recognizing how our parents would often use their humor to make a needed point. By doing this, they would lessen the emotional trauma our actions had caused.

My mother's philosophy on life was: "Don't take yourself too seriously. If you do take yourself too seriously, you will miss out on the fun of life." Mom believed that life had enough ups and downs without adding to them by taking life too seriously.

My mother was also a child of the Depression. She lost her father at the age of three and certainly knew her share of heartache and stress. For a short time her and her siblings lived in a children's home in High Point, North Carolina. My grandmother was trying to learn an occupation that would support her and three children. This was the Depression; lives were altered. But my mother never lost her love of life and her appreciation of laughter and a smile. I can safely say my mother never hesitated to laugh at herself or even use self-deprecating humor in her efforts to generate laughter with others. A great lesson I learned from my mother was that life may be serious but it need not be taken too seriously.

Surviving some of life's challenges may be as simple as allowing yourself to smile and have some fun. On these long trips across America, Mom would attempt to scale down some of Dad's tall tales but she too enjoyed the stories. Mom never hesitated to use her wonderful sense humor as she tried to educate and entertain Barry and I. That was the lesson learned from Mom and Dad: If you allow for laughter and you project a smile you are going to be better equipped for whatever life throws at you.

One of my favorite stories about Mom's willingness to laugh at herself happened on a family trip to southwest Texas. We were traveling with Mom's sister Nancy and her family. This in itself provided laughter considering we had five children and four adults traveling in one car. Of course, the cars were much larger in those days. As was the norm, our family stopped at a roadside attraction, on the outskirts of El Paso. While visiting this outpost of entertainment, Daddy thought it would be funny if he could get a photo of Mom pretending to sit on a cactus (here, the key word is pretending); need I say more? This photo-op would turn especially funny when my mother lost her balance and fell posterior-first into the thorny plant. It was impossible not to laugh as she sat in the cactus. Fortunately, we learned she was not hurt as her facial expression turned from fear to laughter. When she started laughing everyone felt free to laugh as well. My mother was able to show us firsthand the importance of laughing at one's self. The absurdities of this mishap led to our family sharing laughter about the event for years to come. Indeed my father was able to catch the action on film and when those photos were developed our family once again shared a laugh. The story soon developed a life of its own and became known as "Mom's great cactus adventure" and the story and pictures were shared with others for many years.

Since my father's death and with my mother's advancing age I take a great deal of comfort remembering these special times. These were times that our family shared love and laughter. Through the good and bad, laughter was a constant. While growing up I may not have known the importance of laughter but I did enjoy it. As I look back now, I recognize how important laughter was for everyone. Our laughter served as a tonic which helped combat stress and gave us a great deal of enjoyment. All of which helped create a strong family bond that has served me well for over 50 years and helped make me the person I am today.

Chapter 2

The Fuel for Lifelong Laughter

Children have a special ability to create their own entertainment—maybe by running through a sprinkler, or having a snowball fight (hopefully not on the same day). When you see a child at play you also witness the child's creative spirit. If you spend any time watching children at play you can't miss the magic and the laughter. Children of all ages have the ability to communicate through laughter.

Unfortunately, too often in adulthood our childhood spirit is lost. As adults our outlook is affected by deadlines, mortgages, car payments, health problems and any number of other stressors. All stressors can contribute to a deficiency of laughter. Without laughter we may find ourselves in a "Catch 22" of less laughter, more stress, more stress, less laughter. All of this can contribute to an unhealthy lifestyle. It's important to recognize the importance of laughter to a balanced life.

"If you lose the power to laugh you lose the power to think."
—Clarence Darrow

Sometimes we need to go backward in order to move forward. By this I am talking of recognizing what made you smile as a child, remembering the fun activities that produced laughter. When we recall these memories we will be better equipped in our efforts to rediscover our childhood laughter. These memories may also give us some insight into the way we live today. No matter where we are in life we can always benefit from a refresher course in laughter. Life is much more enjoyable when it includes laughter.

My recognition of the value of laughter has positively influenced my life and the lives of my loved ones. The knowledge that a good dose of laughter could well be the secret to positive emotions and a good life, led me to write this book. I wanted to put down on paper how laughter not only has impacted my life but that it is also a resource that is available to everyone.

When I first thought about writing this book I realized I needed to review how laughter had affected my life over the years. When I started the review process it didn't take long for me to recognize the fact that laughter is and has been a major part of my life both professionally and socially.

When I realized that retail management was not in my future I decided to enter the wonderful world of counseling. My first counseling job was with an employment agency in Winston Salem, N.C. My responsibilities were simple: help match clients with suitable employment opportunities. I was young and naive and really not sure what to expect. I soon learned that no matter what the position or what the duties, if you are open to humor you will find humor. Humor can be found everywhere—especially if you deal with people on a personal level.

I had only been with the agency a few weeks when a client came into my office proclaiming, "I *want a job looking good and paying good."* Is this not everybody's dream job? I told him that desire may present a problem if such a job existed; we would both be competing for the position. Who doesn't want a job looking good paying good? Every day I dealt with a wide range of people all looking for work—blue collar and white collar. I realized that no matter what their background or qualifications, our interaction was always better when we could share some laughter.

"The human race has only one really effective weapon and that is laughter."

—Mark Twain

Time and time again I was reminded of a line from a Waylon Jennings song, *"Ain't no ordinary dude don't have to work. Got my name painted on my shirt."* Such was the observation of a young employment counselor. My humor not only helped me in the interview process but it also helped build positive relationships with employers and clients alike. Laughter was something we could share no matter what the circumstance.

After two years of working as an employment counselor, my career path took me in a different direction. I decided to go into the behavioral health field. I moved to South Carolina and accepted a position as an alcohol and drug abuse counselor. At this time I also decided to pursue a master's degree in counseling. My theory on laughter was beginning to take shape as I began to realize that my educational and professional development would be enhanced by a good sense of humor. I continued to work as a counselor in the addictions field after finishing my master's degree in counselor education.

As an addictions counselor I conducted group and individual therapy sessions. I'm not sure how many clients I actually helped, but I tried. Truth is, I probably benefited more from these sessions than the patients. I was learning a lot about myself and life. Visitors to the hospital often would ask how one could tell the patients from the staff. Our standard response was that the patients got better. One of the main lessons I learned as an addictions counselor was the value of a positive attitude. Our attitude affects everything we do and if we maintain a positive attitude then we will have greater control over negative situations.

If you can develop an attitude that allows you to laugh at yourself through bad times and good, it will produce tremendous health benefits. One of the main benefits however is a healthy, happy lifestyle. Laughter gives us a wonderful perspective on life and its many challenges. During my years at the hospital I learned a lot about human nature. I also learned that a shared laugh can not only improve relationships; it can also go a long way toward an improved life.

"If you laugh at yourself you will always have something to laugh at."

—Author unknown

It was this professional backdrop that led me to the development of presentations and workshops that became known as "Better Living through Laughter." These workshops are an extension of my belief that laughter is a vital resource for life. It's no secret that I consider laughter a very important part of my life. I am a firm believer that laughter should be a part of everyone's life—every day.

Probably the best compliment my daughter Lila ever gave me was the day she said, *"Daddy you laugh all the time."* I certainly try to laugh every day. My hope is as she ages she will remember to laugh every day and with her laughter, she will think of her dad.

Chapter 3

I'm laughing, now what?

Though I recognized the value of laughter, it was not until I became director of staff development for our hospital that I became interested in sharing my beliefs on humor professionally. One of my responsibilities within this position was to keep up with national trends and theories concerning addictions and treatment. I would review professional journals and articles addressing treatment modalities and issues. One article that I came across intrigued me. The article put forth the theory that the most effective counselors in the addictions field were the ones with less than two years experience. The article rationalized that counselors who were new to the field were less likely to be affected by the stress of the profession. The author felt counselors with more seniority were more vulnerable to occupational stress and thus become less effective in their counseling efforts. In addition, the article theorized that a counselor with less than two years of experience not only benefited from being somewhat naive but that he or she also had more energy for the demands of the position.

The demands were not physical but mental in nature. Of course my first reaction to this theory was to laugh—how could one be so wrong! I was into my eighth year as a counselor and felt fairly confident. That being said, I also realized that with any occupation there is always potential for burnout and complacency.

Every day our counselors were called on to help clients recognize and deal with the negative choices they had made in their lives. In group therapy and individual therapy sessions the counselors would help address the behaviors that led the client to be self-destructive in their use of alcohol and other drugs. Counselors were called on to help the clients find an alternative to their self-destructive behaviors and encourage them to change their lifestyles.

Counselors also helped clients establish treatment goals that would address the addictive behavior of the client. The hope was that these goals would help lead each client to a life of sobriety. It was not uncommon for the goals to be rejected by the client forcing the counselor into additional roles that ranged from cheerleader to an authority figure and even to a friend. Many times all the roles were required when it came to helping the client develop a new approach to life. It was not unusual for the counselor to have a high emotional investment. The journal article theorized that all of this emotional investment would leave the counselor predisposed to stress and burnout, resulting in less effective therapy.

I never really bought into this theory. I felt my experience made me a better counselor and gave me a greater sense of the needs of the position and the years of experience helped me avoid burnout by not allowing myself to be manipulated or played by the client. Though I was in disagreement with the article it did cause some personal and professional curiosity. I decided to review our hospital's approach to patient care and the interactions of the clinicians and support staff. I was hoping to learn whether there was a burnout problem or not. If burnout did exist, I needed to know to what extent and if it adversely affected the treatment program.

I did what any good staff development person would do: I took a survey. I was hoping to find out how the staff felt about the hospital's programs and their personal responsibilities. I was looking for the good, the bad and the ugly.

Though the questionnaire had many parts, the part that garnered the most attention prompted: *"Identify one thing that would help you feel better about your job and your professional development."* Most of the answers focused on the expectations of the job. Some were looking for a decrease in paper work or asking for an increase in staff support. Environmental changes were suggested and of course the most popular response was the need for more money. All of this would require the action of someone with a much higher paid grade. I was unable to address any of these suggestions. Fortunately, there was one concern identified that I could address: the need for a program on stress management.

In our hospital, stress was definitely alive and well. Shortly before I took the survey the hospital had gone through some stressful events including budget cuts and increased workloads. And everyone was dealing with possible lay-offs. It was no wonder the staff felt overworked and unappreciated. Each new demand brought on greater insecurity, increasing the stress levels of everyone. This all contributed to the staff having negative feelings about their jobs.

All professions have built in stressors and the behavioral health field is no different. It doesn't take a brain surgeon to realize that if stress is left unchecked it will negatively affect the job. I felt if we didn't address the levels of stress at the hospital it would have a negative impact on treatment and hospital operations.

"If you can't make it better you have to laugh at it."
—Erma Bombeck

With survey results in hand I turned my attention to the development of a stress management program. At first I studied traditional approaches to stress management which included meditation with deep-breathing exercises. The focus of these exercises was to help the participants learn to take a mental break from perceived stress. The breathing exercises focused on relaxation increasing the oxygen intake while relaxing the body. These exercises were designed to help the participants learn additional ways to relax. From my studies I hoped to create a program that would not only help with stress but also help to identify and address the warning signs of stress. I was hoping the staff could begin addressing their stress as a group. If we worked together everyone would have a part in the management of hospital stress. The more I learned about stress management, the more I realized that it was an avenue for self-care. I felt that good stress management gives us the ability to put the brakes on what could be perceived as a runaway train. Or at least help the train stay on its tracks.

Most traditional stress management courses asked the participants to visualize a calm and peaceful place. As you visualize your peaceful place, you are asked to do some deep-breathing exercises. The intake of oxygen helps cleanse the mind and relax the body. As you begin to relax the perceived stress becomes less powerful and you begin to gain some control over your emotional state.

When I led these stress management courses I certainly recognized the benefits of these techniques. But the more I looked at my own stress I began to realize what worked for me was laughter. When I laughed I felt better mentally and physically. I knew that laughter had helped me deal with many a runaway train in my life. I also knew that a simple laugh goes a long way toward the reduction of stress and tension. My laughter allowed me to gain a healthier attitude and an improved outlook. I began to believe that everyone should be able to benefit from a good laugh—after all, everyone is capable of laughter and laughter positively affects many aspects of life.

When I laugh I become more relaxed. It makes little difference what the situation is—if I can laugh, I am better equipped for the challenge. With humor I gain greater flexibility in my approach to life. I have more control over my emotions and actions when I allow for laughter. Laughter helps put things in perspective—a perspective that I can deal with. When you have control over your emotions you are better equipped to handle your stressors and non-stressors alike.

Of course, the use of humor is more than laughing and telling jokes. Humor is a positive resource for our health and well being. Helping us gain a positive outlook and attitude. The old saying, *"Let a smile be your umbrella,"* is more than a saying—it can be a rule to live by.

I knew that everyone has the ability to laugh so it seemed only appropriate that I turn my attention to the utilization of humor as a tool for stress management. My hope was to develop a program that not only addressed stress management but also helped participants rediscover the joy of laughter and its many benefits. My early studies focused on the affects of laughter and its effects on our emotional and physical health. I wanted everyone to learn that a simple laugh goes a long way in how it affects us mentally and physically. Finding truth in the philosophy, *"laughter is the best medicine."*

Personally I have found one of the biggest benefits of laughter to be the way it helps me gain acceptance over the things I cannot change. If you can accept the challenge you can do something about it. Too often we find ourselves in emotional ruts trying to change things we have no control over. Everyone is affected by situations we seem to have little or no control over. This lack of control can make us angry and frustrated. Rather than surrendering to events we have no control over, we need to step back and recognize what we do have control over. No matter the situation, we always have control over our attitude. The truth is, our attitude is the only thing we have absolute control over period. If we take control of our attitude then we can begin to control our stress and our emotions. Taking control over our attitude will give us greater power in dealing with negative events in our life.

Trouble arises when we allow outside influences to control our attitude. When this happens we get caught up in the negative—giving way to anger and frustration. With anger and frustration comes an increase in stress. If you give up control of your attitude then you are setting the stage for all types of problems.

Negative stress is a part of life everyone experiences. How we are affected by stressful events comes down to our attitude. It is important to recognize that stress and pain are unavoidable. They are a part of life. But we do have some options as to how we handle them. One of the options is to look for joy and happiness. If we relinquish control over our attitude we will begin losing control over other events in life. The perceived thought of being out of control is one of the most powerful causes of emotional illnesses and problems we can experience. Lack of control over our emotions will adversely affect our physical and mental well-being. It's hard to enjoy life if you feel out of control.

"One of the best things to have up your sleeve, is a funny bone."
—Author unknown

A way to overcome feelings of helplessness is to start using your sense of humor and rediscover the value of a good laugh. When we begin to use our sense of humor productively we will soon discover that laughter can be found everywhere. Survivors of natural disasters often talk about how their faith and sense of humor helped them survive. A good dose of laughter may indeed be the first step to a better life.

Is laughter the best medicine? Well, if it's not the best medicine, then one must consider it a close second. Research shows that experiencing laughter and having a positive mental attitude can produce a healing effect on the body and the soul. A good hardy belly laugh helps release endorphins—the brain's natural painkiller. Endorphins also help bolster the body's immune system helping ward off disease and stress. Not only does a good laugh serve the mind well but it also does wonders for us physically. Laughter increases our intake of oxygen and while we are laughing our muscles get a good workout. This helps strengthen the heart and increases the flow of blood. Good things happen when you laugh. So for many, laughter is the best medicine. Laughter will help us discover a positive outlook for life and is a marvelous resource for mental and physical health.

Chapter 4

Some Humor Sense
Sense of Humor Magic

Everyone has some basic needs. They may include the need to be loved, the need to feel secure, the need for faith as well as the need for food and water. Another need is the need of laughter. *The need for laughter*? Yes; the need for laughter. The need for laughter may be as basic as the need to breath. If we consider the many benefits of laughter it's understandable why I would refer to laughter as one of our basic needs. Laughter has so many benefits that affect us physically, mentally and spiritually. Laughter provides an emotional release that affects our attitude and our disposition—both of which are extremely important in life.

If it has been awhile since you enjoyed a good hearty laugh you may need to ask yourself why. If you are not laughing you are missing out on a wonderful resource for health and wellness. While enjoying a good laugh the entire body gets a workout. The benefits can be felt from head to toe.

You may need to look at what's preventing you from taking a mental break or enjoying a short laughter workout? Have you forgotten the benefits of laughter? Does life seem less enjoyable? Maybe all you need to do is rediscover the things that created laughter in the past. It's important to rediscover laughter to allow for laughter to take place.

The quality of one's life can be defined by their attitude and how well they get along with others. This is true at work, in the home and in his or her community. One's attitude sets the stage for how we deal with life's victories as well as its defeats. Most people are judged by their attitude. An attitude is that powerful. We are attracted to people with pleasant attitudes. Shared laughter only enhances attitudes and the attraction. Laughter can promote good feelings and positive actions if enjoyed properly.

No one would readily admit they don't have a sense of humor. After all, a sense of humor is considered an admirable trait and is desired by many. Yet everyone can identify someone they feel has little or no sense of humor. Survey a 100 people, ask them if they know someone without a sense of humor and the overwhelming answer would be yes. They quickly begin identifying co-workers, friends and family members. Almost everyone knows someone who is probably suffering from a bad case of terminal seriousness. Terminal seriousness is a disease that can affect individuals' corporations and communities. When someone is suffering from terminal seriousness they may believe demonstrating a sense of humor is a sign of immaturity and possibly shows a lack of professionalism. For these individuals, it indicates a lack of an appreciation for life. Maybe their mantra for life should be, *"Humor, we don't need no stinking humor!"* Their belief is that life is serious and needs to be taken seriously. I will agree that life is indeed serious, but it is much too serious to take seriously.

Life is too Serious to take Seriously

A good sense of humor allows us the freedom to share laughter. Everyone can benefit from a sense of humor no matter what direction life takes them. Those who suffer from terminal seriousness may need to cultivate their sense of humor a little more and begin enjoying the laughter that comes with it. They will soon discover the many benefits that laughter brings and their lives will be enhanced professionally, socially and spiritually.

Some *"Serious Sams"* just lack the confidence to use their humor. Fearing their humor is not up to par with others, they likely suffer from a case of humor envy. Humor is an individual trait. Don't look at it as a competitive sport. Life is not an episode of *"The Last Comic Standing."* Just relax and enjoy it. Don't get caught up in who is funnier or funniest.

We need to recognize our personal humor quota and become comfortable with its usage. Then we should start using and enjoying our humor. Once we have discovered our own comfort level for humor, we can begin putting it to work. With usage, our humor potential will increase and we will find ourselves becoming more and more humorous. Much like the snowball rolling down the snowy hill—it will grow. The more we use it the more it will grow and the more it grows the better equipped we will become to share it.

Even the *Serious Sams* of the world were born with the ability to enjoy laughter. Why they have chosen not to use their humor and to take on a non- humorous attitude for life is anyone's bet. No matter what the reason for terminal seriousness there is a cure and the cure can be found, once again, in our attitude. By developing an attitude that allows for laughter and joy we can begin realizing the magic of laughter that we once enjoyed as children.

We develop the ability to laugh early in life. Freud was one of the first to study laughter, he believed that laughter began with the smile of a content baby and increased as the child aged. David Cohen Ph.D., a British psychologist, has researched the personal growth of laughter in children and he believes that infants begin laughing around nine weeks of age. At first, the child may smile indiscriminately at bodily functions. But with age comes the ability to recognize external stimulations. Maybe the stimulation comes from a parent or a loved one stimulating the child to laugh or giggle. As children begin developing the ability to communicate and laugh, their laughter will increase. When children become more aware of their world laughter continues to develop. Around 10 months of age, a child may begin seeing their environment as a playground for laughter. Maybe their laughter is a result of a parent making a funny face or someone performing a comical act. The child is becoming more aware of physical, visual and auditory stimulations that can lead to the development of laughter.

With age comes the ability to not only share laughter, but create it as well. A child's laughter will continue to grow becoming a regular component of their developing life. It will increase to the point that by the time a child reaches the age of four they may actually be laughing an average of once every four minutes. Once every four minutes, is a tremendous amount of laughter. This compared to the average adult who laughs an average of 15 times a day presents quite a contrast. So what happens to these young comedians, and why do they begin to experience less laughter? What contributes to laughter taking a back seat in our development?

One possible reason for the decline in laughter could relate to the child's development as they grow older. Soon after the age of four, school begins and with school comes a new set of expectations and goals. During the early years, the child begins identifying needs and goals associated with personal and physical development resulting in perceived stress. With perceived stress the child begins to lose control and the stress grows contributing to a void in the use of humor. Unfortunately children are not immune to stress and its negative consequences.

How we use our sense of humor can be an indication to the view we have of life. Even though we are born with the foundation for a sense of humor, its development is dependent on what type of stimuli and situations we encounter as we age. One's personal mental health can be greatly affected by how they view and live life and use their sense of humor. If life is viewed as a constant challenge and/or struggle, then we are less likely to use our sense of humor. If our approach to life includes laughter and joy then we have a greater foundation for growing our sense of humor. No matter what one's personal rate of laughter is, there is always room for improvement and it can be improved by recognizing the value of laughter.

Our lifestyle and outlook will improve as we recognize the value of a good laugh. We may not be laughing once every four minutes, but most likely we do laugh more than we eat. No matter our age or situation laughter is always beneficial. Everyone can benefit from a good laugh. Laughter has no age limit and it doesn't require any money. It is free to anyone who looks for it. A chuckle can go a long way toward enhancing our personal development. A positive goal would be to increase our laughter to the point that it becomes a regular part of our life—as normal as breathing.

I personally consider laughter the miracle drug of the new millennium. A good laugh helps in all areas of life. Research shows that a good strong belly laugh that last for three minutes will have the same affect on the body internally as 20 minutes of exercise on a rowing machine. Which would you prefer? Mentally, laughter can improve our disposition while contributing to a positive outlook helping in the reduction of stress and anxiety. Even a small chuckle can produce positive side effects.

For us to a gain a better appreciation of laughter and the value of using our sense of humor, we should first define "humor." After we have arrived at our definition we should begin applying it. Our sense of humor enables us to laugh, communicate and enjoy life. The word humor itself has many meanings. The root of the word is "umor" meaning liquid or fluid. In ancient times humor referred to bodily fluids and was viewed as the state of health of the individual. One in bad health was often referred to as being in bad humor. Today, bad humor may not reflect the physical well being of an individual but can be a reflection of one's attitude.

Webster's dictionary describes humor as "the mental faculty of discovering expressing, or appreciating the ludicrous or absurdity of an incongruous situation". In layman's terms, it is the ability to have fun. A good sense of humor is the key to laughter and this is important because laughter, after all, is the best medicine. If we are laughing then we are enjoying life more. Another benefit is the positive view our peers and coworkers will have of us when they see us using our humor in a productive fashion. A good sense of humor can make the difference between success and failure.

In summary, laughter can be an effective tool for self-care as well as self-development. Humor and laughter help create and strengthen a positive and hopeful attitude.

Could I have Humor in my Environment?

Instructions: Read the statements and rate your humor environment.
1. Rarely/Never   2. At Times   3. No Opinion   4. Often   5. Very Often

1. _____I often hear laughter at work.

2. _____I will initiate laughter with co-workers.

3. _____My curiosity arises when I hear laughter.

4. _____I enjoy a good laugh.

5. _____My parents shared their sense of humor.

6. _____There is laughter in my house.

7. _____I enjoy creating things.

8. _____My sense of humor helps me deal with difficult people.

9. _____I can be called on to share a joke.

10. _____When I experience something funny I will share it with others.

11. _____My friends and loved ones would consider my sense of humor an assist.

12. _____I am a humor consumer.

13. _____I collect humorous items.

14. _____When alone I still find myself laughing.

15. _____I look for humor.

If you scored between 66-75: you have got your humor working. 45-65: a slight humor tune up may be needed. 28-44: we are talking overhaul. Exercise your sense of humor—find something funny quick. Under 28: you are in dire straits and may need a humor transplant.

"*Mooing*"
Away
Stress

Moo!

Chapter 5

Fighting Stress with Laughter!

As mentioned earlier, my study of laughter began after I recognized how I used my humor in my personal battles with stress. I feel fortunate that I discovered early on the value of a good laugh and the positive side effects it had on me personally and professionally. When I'm confronted with stressful events or situations, my humor gives me a healthier perspective. Through my laughter my attitude improves and I gain greater control over my emotions.

In some traditional stress management programs participants are called on to visualize a calm and peaceful place while practicing deep breathing exercises. I did not question the value of such exercises; I was concerned that it may not have the long-term benefits needed. It is always beneficial to take time for yourself and the deep breathing mediation allows you to do this. My question was: does it really give us a handle on the stress or is it just a temporary fix?

The solution being presented in these sessions was to visualize a trip to the coast accompanied by deep breathing. Sure, it may be beneficial and it does produce a mental break from stress. The problem I saw was that in most cases when the exercise concluded, the stress remained. If this was the case, then the participants were not gaining control over their perception of the stressful event. (It's important to remember that stress is not the result of an event—it is our perception of the event.) This led me to realize that a key to stress reduction is as simple as managing our perception, and if you could control your perception you could control your stress. My friend Bob has a saying: "What the mind perceives the body receives." If our mind sees it we will feel it. Think about this statement: What the mind sees the body receives. If we are feeling down, our body language will reflect it; if we are feeling positive and energetic, then our body language will indicate this as well. More important than body language is how our mind reflects our feeling. If you are thinking how miserable things are then you are going to feel the misery. The same can be said for stressful events. If we see stress and interpret it negatively, then our body will communicate negatively. So, perception management is indeed a form of stress management.

> **"Don't sweat the petty things and don't pet the sweaty things."**
> **—George Carlin**

I discovered that by using my humor I gained greater control over my perception and attitude and this, in turn, enabled me to have greater control over my stress. This has led me to try and see the humor in the events that may give me stressful feelings. I know that laughter helps reduce my personal and professional stress. For me a simple laugh goes a long way toward the reduction of negative stress and tension, and to top it off, it just makes me feel better. Laughter allows me to face stressful events and situations with greater relaxation and ease.

Speech teachers tell reluctant students that if they are having trouble with their nerves when it comes to addressing a large group they should imagine everyone in the audience sitting in their underwear. After the speaker has pictured this humorous sight in their mind they can proceed to give the speech. The theory is: if your audience is dressed only in their underwear how critical can they be and how serious can the situation be? This is a classic example of how to change your perception. The humorous notion of everyone being in their underwear helps reduce the tension and stress of the moment. This is a different form of using humor. We are not telling jokes or sharing laughter but we are using humor to redirect our thought patterns. This is a reflection of how we face certain challenges in life. I have found the use of humor gives me greater flexibility when dealing with stressful situations. That is the ultimate payoff of a good laugh—we gain greater control over life's challenges.

Psychologist Lisa Rosenberg says, "Humor is not just laughing at a joke. It is a perception of life." Humor is an emotional release that allows us to continue functioning in stressful situations. Our laughter helps dispel negative emotions, and helps create a frame of mind that allows for better coping skills. Sometimes our efforts to find humor may only result in a quick smile or a funny reflection, but the benefits are tenfold. It's simple: a change in your perception can lower your stress and humor can give us that change in perception.

Stress has been described by Hans Selye, a pioneer in the research of psychosomatic medicine, as: "the rate of wear and tear within the body" (*refer to Stress Man Chart as to the adverse effects of stress on page 40*) as the body adapts to change or threats. This wear and tear is not only physical but emotional as well. Uncontrolled stress can produce feelings of malaise and indifference. If we fail to control our stress we may find ourselves in an emotional rut—feeling out of control with little hope for a better tomorrow. There is an old country song that helps describe the emotional rut one gets into when stress takes over To paraphrase the lyrics: "*Why must tomorrow be today all over again?*" If we find ourselves in emotional ruts, then our tomorrows will be repeats of our todays.

> **"I've got a new philosophy...
> I only dread one day at a time."**
>
> —Charlie Brown

"Stress Man" illustrates how individuals may respond to stress in a variety of ways. Reponses may be psychological, physical or behavioral. Our response to stress is largely dependent on our vulnerability at the time. If we are confident in our ability to successfully deal with the situation then our reaction to the stress will be minimal. In turn, the more vulnerable we are the more likely it is that we will be negatively affected by the stressful events. Uncontrolled stress can result in a depletion of our immune system promoting greater wear and tear on our body and mind. Common problems related to stress identified by *Stress Man* may include ulcers, headaches and high blood pressure. The higher our stress level, the greater the negative consequences. There is a direct correlation between stress and almost every disease. Unchecked stress may also cause diseases to advance—making recovery more difficult. Emotionally stress can lead to anxiety and nervousness resulting in poor sleep habits and the depletion of personal energy. If we find ourselves with little energy then we may feel our "get up and go" got up and went.

Stress can also affect our gastrointestinal tract resulting in poor digestion, constipation or diarrhea. The negative effects go on and on including how it can affect our cardiovascular system by contributing to poor blood flow. It is clear that stress can affect us physically and mentally. It is important to recognize how vulnerable we are to stress. Does stress cause an increase in headaches and stomach pain? Or maybe it is causing us to lose sleep or become hyperactive. Once we begin recognizing how stress affects us it becomes imperative that we develop a strategy that helps address stress and its affects. A successful stress management strategy can be crucial to the development of a healthy lifestyle.

When stressed, the brain goes into the 'fight or flight syndrome.' The message the body receives is that it's time to take action. Initially the body's response may be a quickening of the pulse, accompanied by shallow breathing with an increase in muscle tension. When this takes place the body will begin producing adrenaline, the hormone that gives us the physical and emotional feeling of being stressed.

One of the more popular characters on the old "Andy Griffith Show" was Ernest T. Bass. Bass was somewhat of a recluse who often would come down from the hills seeking love and adventure and always causing problems. Known for speaking in rhymes, Ernest T. was known to say, "If you don't run from fright, I'm here to fight." When Ernest T. was around you can bet the citizens of Mayberry were feeling more than a little stress. But at least he was giving them fair warning. Ernest T. was delivering his own fight or flight message. We will all be better off if we can begin recognizing our own "Ernest T.'s,"—those things that lead to our fight or flight reactions.

Unfortunately not all our stressors are as kind. We may not recognize it at first but if we know how our body and mind react to stress then we can develop the skills and techniques for good stress management. Ernest T. gave the warning and Andy and Barney would always come up with solutions. Everyone should have an action plan for dealing with their personal Ernest T.'s.

Stress probably needs a good public relations firm, because not all stress is bad. The reasons we get up in the morning to go to work and carry out a normal day are a result of stress. It's a natural part of our life. Stress is a necessity of life. One only becomes stress-free with death. If this is the case, I will gladly accept a little stress. It is not how much stress we have but how we handle the stress we have. A good coping mechanism will give us greater control over stress rather than having stress control us.

It's not how much stress we have but how we handle the stress we have.

In my own version of "Family Feud," I surveyed 100 people asking: *"What would you do if you were approached by an angry bear?"* The overwhelming number one answer was: "run." Few people want to wait and analyze the situation and then take a course of action. Sometimes unwanted stress may feel like we are being confronted by an angry bear—we want to run. Unfortunately running is seldom a viable option. If you can't run from stress, what options do you have? The best option is to develop your own defense mechanism that helps in managing stress. Stress can come at us from all areas of life—at work, in the home or on the highway. It knows no barriers!

Everyone is faced with their own deadlines. From racing time clocks to shopping for gifts, even some of the simplest tasks can produce negative stress. When negative stress becomes too common we can feel overwhelmed and maybe a little out of control. In a recent Gallup poll, 40% of the population said they felt negative stress every day. Another 39% felt it often. With figures like these it is easy to understand that stress is a normal part of life and something everyone must deal with. Most of our stressors are not going to be as easy to recognize as the angry bear, but for many, the consequences can be just as traumatic. No matter how the stress is introduced, the results are all too familiar. Refer once again to *Stress Man*. It becomes increasingly important that we develop a personal self-care program that helps in the reduction of stress or at least gives us greater control over how our body reacts to it. By developing a program that addresses stress, the consequences should be less damaging.

Personally my best defense mechanism has been and remains the use of humor and laughter. Laughter gives me the tools and confidence to confront stressful situations with greater control. I have found that when I use my humor I am able to set the stage for possible resolutions to the stress or, at least, its management. Most of the time this helps me avoid the physical and mental pitfalls that are reflected by *Stress Man*.

Why does laughter work? Think about your own use of laughter and how you feel after a good laugh. Laughter helps us relax which gives us a change of perception that ultimately results in a better attitude. To hammer home an earlier statement, stress is the result of our perception of an event. When we utilize our sense of humor and enjoy a good laugh we gain greater control over our attitude and our perceptions. Laughter may not be a cure-all for stress, but it can certainly have a positive effect to how we deal with it. We have all heard the philosophy of life that says, "Don't sweat the small stuff and you will find out that it's all small stuff." If we are honest with ourselves we may realize that the cause of our stress may actually fall into the small stuff category. Humorous outlooks can possibly keep these stressors in the small stuff category. When facing adversity, if we can find some humor in the situation or possibly from another source, it can and will help with our attitude and allow us to gain greater control over our emotions and actions. Humor will supply some flexibility that can be priceless when stress becomes overbearing.

That is why laughter and humor are valuable resources in the battle of stress. Laughter helps dispel negative emotions, putting us in a better frame of mind to cope with the cards life deals us. When you get lemons, make lemonade. Freud was one of the first clinicians to view humor as a healthy means of coping with stress. Over a century ago, he pointed out the value of laughter and how important it was for one to use their sense of humor. He felt laughter was a positive response to life's challenges. He believed it gave us greater control over our environment in addition to helping clear the mind from negative and destructive thought patterns.

George Valliant, in the book *Adaptation to Life*—which poses fundamental questions about individual differences in confronting stress—reported that humor has been identified as an effective tool for the management of on-the-job stress. In other studies, Vera Robinson, on the faculty of California State University in Fullerton has done an extensive study concerning the use of humor by healthcare professionals. She has determined that laughter has a positive influence on our physical and emotional health. With laughter comes the ability to adapt. It will also help prevent the internalization of stress—thus reducing the risk for stress-related illnesses.

We are confronted with potential stressors daily. In the words of Gilda Radnor as Roseanna Roseanna Danna of "Saturday Night Live," "It's always something!" The event may set the stage for stress but our perceptions make it negative. Similar to the computer term 'garbage in garbage out,' the same can be said for our attitude. If we continue to allow garbage into our attitude, our attitude is going to reflect that garbage.

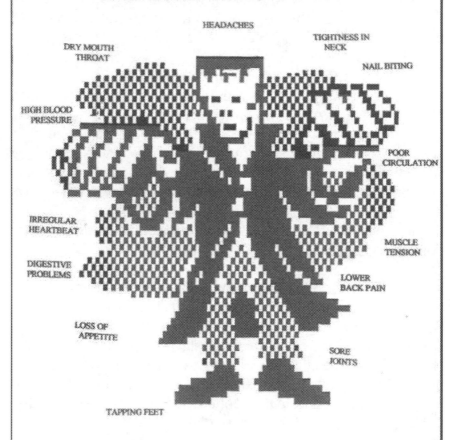

STRESS MAN

HEADACHES

TIGHTNESS IN
NECK

DRY MOUTH
THROAT

NAIL BITING

HIGH BLOOD
PRESSURE

POOR
CIRCULATION

IRREGULAR
HEARTBEAT

MUSCLE
TENSION

DIGESTIVE
PROBLEMS

LOWER
BACK PAIN

LOSS OF
APPETITE

SORE
JOINTS

TAPPING FEET

 Many of these symptoms accompany stress.
Are you a stress man?

Just Add Humor
P.O. Box 210503
Columbia, S.C. 29210

One way of gaining a better understanding of the power of perception can be seen in how we deal with a simple traffic jam. Imagine you are in a traffic jam; all you see is a sea of red lights in what appears to be the world's largest parking lot. Now consider how you react to such an event. Think about this scenario as you approach the sea of red lights. You apply the brakes and the traffic stops or proceeds slowly, and you begin processing the event. Your leisurely drive has the potential to turn into a stressful event as traffic moves at a snail's pace. The only way to change lanes is to trade cars with the guy next to you. At first you may be a little inquisitive as to the cause of the delay; you feel concern hoping there has not been an accident. Early on while in the traffic jam your thoughts are of others—not of yourself, but as time begins to slip away your mind becomes flooded with approaching deadlines and thoughts of where you need to be. You start thinking less about the event and more about all the things you need to get done. Your concern has been replaced by frustration and anger as you wonder what could possibly be causing such a delay. Your mood is shifting—you have crossed over from being concern to being stressed out. The longer you are in the traffic jam the more negative you become. As your mood shifts, your stress level escalates.

Your breathing has become shallower and you have developed tightness in your stomach. You are feeling tension in your arms and legs. You begin gripping the steering wheel tighter and tighter with each passing minute. You have reached the point where the traffic jam has become a major source of stress. Not only are you experiencing physical stress, your mental state is not doing all that well either.

Your attitude has been adversely affected. While you sit in this parking lot with a 65 mph speed limit your anger escalates. You openly dare drivers to try and get in your lane your and driving become a little more reckless and aggressive—all in response to your perception of the traffic jam. You have gone from thinking, "Oh I hope no one is hurt," to "Their better be blood on the highway." The traffic jam has produced stress and it is taking its toll both physically and emotionally. Anger and frustration have replaced concern. The fight or flight syndrome has taken hold but there is nowhere to run and the only fighting you are doing is with the steering wheel. You have surrendered control over your emotions and how you view the traffic jam. No longer in control the traffic jam has taken control of you. In a short period of time your mood has been altered and you feel very different. Unchecked stress has found another victim. Your mental and physical conditions are being affected every time you apply the brakes.

Now let's look at this same event and, rather than stew on the negative, try to change our perceptions with the use of a little humor. Again, remember it's not the event but our reaction to the event that matters. The next time you are faced with slow or non-moving traffic, simply put your humor to work. When the highway, turns into a parking lot, begin looking around seeking out things that could be considered humorous. You may find it in billboards or you may find it in a vanity plate on the rolling wreck beside you. Maybe a good laugh can be found in someone's bumper sticker or someone's hairdo. What's important is to look anywhere and everywhere for humor. Look for the incongruence that may be present in the situation. We are decreasing our stress and anxiety by finding laughter in the stressful world.

Another way of changing our perception of the traffic jam may be found in an adaptation of a children's game many of us played as kids. We often counted cows in pastures as we made long uneventful trips with our parents. Making a game of counting cows helped us pass the time, but more than just counting cows, we had certain rules that applied. If we passed a cemetery, we would have to "bury" our cows and start over. Or, if we passed a body of water, depending whose side it was on, then that player had to start over because the cows had drown. Cross a train track and it was off to the slaughter house for the cows. Inevitably an offshoot of this game was the desire to communicate with the cows. In time, we would find ourselves doing our best 'moos.' So the next time you are faced with a traffic jam remember this childhood game and think about mooing.

Make eye contact with your neighboring driver, roll down the window and give them your best cow impersonation and 'moo.' I'm betting you will laugh and hopefully the other driver will laugh as well. If not they may well back off and give you the open road. Believe me, it is hard to focus on negative events when you are sharing a moo. The mooing enables us to change our attitude and helps reduce the attention we are paying to the stress and, in this case, the traffic jam. Rather than internalizing and wrestling with our emotions a simple moo gives us some control over how we handle the traffic jam. The traffic jam remains but the difference is in your attitude and your approach. A moo has helped change our perception and we have gained a greater sense of control of our attitude. Controlling our attitude proves beneficial for stress management and anger reduction.

The sea of red taillights remains as well as the slow moving traffic. The only difference is how you are now viewing the predicament. A little mooing reduces our stress and improves our attitude. In this scenario some creative application of humor has reduced the platform for stress.

This simple exercise can be applied to many stressful situations. (When dealing with an angry phone call, put them on hold and moo.) If you have an approaching stressful meeting, take time out to do a moo before joining the meeting. Getting a root canal? Moo beforehand; It's your attitude take control of it.

In many of my workshops I ask participants to identify a stressor in their life and to concentrate on the negative effects of the stress. I have them stand and feel the stress instructing them to squeeze their hands tightly creating tightness in their shoulders and lower back. They feel it in their legs and hands. The tightness will eventually be felt all over the body. When the participants begin to feel and experience the physical complications of the stress they are ready for the exercise.

I refer to the stiffness of the body as the "Frankenstein syndrome." If ever there was a stressed out creature, it was Frankenstein. He was stiff and his joints were always tight. This is why Frankenstein is the model for *Stress Man*. This exercise helps the participants recognize the physical effects of stress. It goes without saying that the exercise is not very pleasant. With all the participants feeling the stress I will then ask them to remember the cow game and to look straight ahead and give their best cow impersonation. I want them to moo and moo again. The moos are usually followed by an outbreak of laughter. The laughter helps the participants loosen up and feel a little less stressed. Overwhelmingly this results in a reduction of tension and stress. One of the main reasons for this reduction is simple—it is difficult to focus on the negative when you change your attitude with a moo.

I did this exercise In a workshop I conducted for a group of managers from the Social Security Administration. I asked the group to identify a stressor in their lives and to feel it both mentally and physically. I then asked them to do a group moo, again explaining the value of changing our perceptions as we deal with stress situations and thoughts. As they mooed they began to laugh and also began to feel better. They enjoyed the exercise and seemed to appreciate the tip for stress management.

One participant wrote to tell me that later in the day, while many of them were waiting on a flight, they put this exercise to work. Their flight was delayed for an extended period of time after they had boarded the plane rendering them trapped on the tarmac. While they waited for take off their stress levels began to climb. With a high level of stress it occurred to them that they should practice what they had learned. First someone in the back of the plane mooed. Then it began to pick up momentum. Soon the entire cabin was laughing and mooing. They were seeing firsthand how a moo can change an attitude. Relief may just be a few moos away! Try it sometime.

Chapter 6

The Prescription is for Laughter
Health and Humor

One of the most notable examples of the value of humor and how it applies to our health can be found in the book *"**Anatomy of an Illness, As Perceived by the Patient: Reflections on Healing Regeneration**"* by Norman Cousins. The book helped introduce the medical community, as well as the world, to the concept that laughter could have a profound effect on disease and wellness. While Cousins was being treated for ankylosing spondylitis, a degenerative spinal condition, he began making some observations that proved invaluable for him as he fought this deadly disease. The disease usually results in acute inflammation affecting the spine and other areas of the body. The attending physicians told Cousins he had little hope for survival or recovery if the disease continued to progress as it had been. Not the information you want from your physician. Suffering from a very painful disease with a poor prognosis, Cousins began to look at all options including some that were not necessarily recognized by the medical community. He theorized that a patient's state of mind played a key role in recovery. From his own experience he soon began to realize the more he thought about his disease, the more pain he experienced. He believed his pain was causing him to be totally preoccupied with the disease and this preoccupation resulted in more pain. He found himself in a vicious cycle— the chronic pain was hindering his recovery, contributing to negative feelings which lead to more pain and discomfort.

This cycle of pain was negatively affecting his attitude and outlook. Fortunately for Cousins, he recognized this negative cycle of emotions and he began to look for ways to redirect his attention. He theorized that if painful thoughts were bringing more pain, the opposite should hold true as well. If he could redirect his attention from the pain to more pleasant thoughts he would theoretically be able to reduce his level of pain. By replacing negative painful thoughts with pleasant or joyful thoughts he would be able to mentally attack the disease resulting in a healthier outlook. After all, he recognized That when he enjoyed time with loved ones and close friends he experienced less pain. These interactions helped redirect his energy—resulting in less pain. Facing his poor prognosis for recovery and with the understanding of his doctors, Cousins left the hospital and began a self-prescribed program, which included the love of his family, his faith, mega-doses of vitamin C and the incorporation of laughter.

In order to stimulate more laughter, he began watching humorous films and television shows from "Candid Camera" to the Marx Brother films. Cousins was stimulating his laughter. Simply put, he believed the more laughter he enjoyed the better he would feel. In his book, he reported making a joyous discovery that 10 minutes of hardy laughter had an anesthetic effect which resulted in his being able to enjoy two hours of pain-free sleep. This was a significant discovery. Laughter, observed Cousins, caused the muscles of the abdomen, chest, shoulders and other areas of the body to contract and his heart rate, respiration rate and blood flow to improve. After a good belly laugh he felt more relaxed and healthier. It did not take long for him to begin seeing the positive effects of his laughter.

His laughter made it easier for him to rest. He indeed discovered that the more he laughed the better he felt. Soon, with his new attitude and with the ability to rest more he began to see a change in his condition. His laughter was paving the way toward an unlikely recovery. Not only did he recover from the illness, he enjoyed an additional 25 years of life! Also, it should be noted that Cousins spent the last 12 years of his life as an Adjunct Professor of Medical Humanities for the School of Medicine at the University of California exploring and researching scientific proof of his beliefs.

If you think about how you feel after a good hardy laugh you can begin seeing how laughter can indeed impact our health. Sometimes you are grasping for air seeking more oxygen; your muscles become loose often to the point that you could easily fall off your chair. Your body is feeling the positive effects of a good laugh. The end result of all the laughter is you just feel better.

The side effects of laughter are positive and numerous. They give us strength and energy for life. When we begin to enjoy the benefits of laughter we become better equipped to face life's challenges. Why not take a laughter vacation? It may be just what the doctor ordered, yielding positive energy and emotions. Laughter is good for everyone. Paraphrasing an American Express ad, one could say, "Humor: Don't leave home without it." When you start enjoying laughter you will discover that the positive energy laughter produces will help in every aspect of your life.

Humor: Don't Leave Home without It!

Since Norman Cousins made his claims regarding the positive effects of laughter, physicians and scientists alike have studied the many benefits of laughter and their research supports Cousins' theories. Dr. William Fry of Stanford University reported that laughter increases respiratory activity, oxygen exchange, muscular activity and heart rate. It stimulates the cardiovascular system, sympathetic nervous system, pituitary gland, and the production of hormones called catecholamines—which in turn stimulate the production of endorphins. The research supports the belief that a good laugh or guffaw is good for the body and the soul. Cousins and Dr. Fry both referred to laughter as internal jogging—the body will benefit from a healthy laugh much like it would benefit from a jog around the block. As with jogging, muscles in the face, arms, legs and stomach will get a work out.

The advantages of internal jogging are many and to top it off—it's safe. You don't have to worry about dogs' traffic or the weather—you can just sit back and laugh. So the next time you are enjoying a good belly laugh and someone wants to know what you are up to, simply tell them that you're jogging and you feel pretty good about it.

Laughing should be seen as a prescription for good health. Let a laughter prescription be your own secret weapon for a healthier lifestyle.

Laughter

A Cure for What Ails You

It's Good Exercise

Energy Efficient

Inflation-Proof

Non-Taxable

It's Healthy

Helps Combat Stress

Improves Blood Circulation

It's a Motivator

Generates Goodwill

The Gift that Keeps on Giving

Share the cure. Enjoy the laughter.

Don't Make WORK a four letter word

Chapter 7

Work doesn't have to be a four-letter word

Today's workforce is continually being asked to do more with less producing increasing feelings of insecurity on the job. For many, this uncertainty has led work to become a major stressor in life. Considering the ever-changing work environment; it is easy to see how a dose of laughter could be beneficial in the workplace.

Many workers are questioning the loyalty of their company and their own future; a stable job is becoming more the exception rather than the rule. With all this uncertainty, the overall work environment is becoming more negative. The vast majorities of today's employees feel unappreciated, overworked and underpaid. With this as the backdrop, it is no wonder that in the U.S. alone workers consume 15 tons of aspirin a day. Fifteen tons of aspirin a day is a lot of aspirin. More employees are being asked to multitask in an effort to get more done with less. Endless workdays contribute to increased time away from family and loved ones, making it more difficult to find healthy outlets for self-care. In the near future it is estimated that job stress will become the number one reason for workers' compensation claims. With increased anxiety comes frustration and exhaustion. The toll of job stress is astronomical affecting production and the overall cost of doing business. Stress also contributes to increased absenteeism, diminished productivity and increased turnover resulting in a cost close to $300 billion annually in the U.S. It is estimated that 60-80% of industrial accidents are the result of on-the-job stress. Worker stress is a problem that needs to be addressed.

Job stress can be defined as the harmful physical and emotional response that occurs when the duties of the job do not match the employee's abilities. Some challenges of the job can be positive leading to the development of new skills and improved abilities. But when a challenge becomes too stressful it could lead to loss of concentration with a decrease in personal productivity. These factors set the stage for job burnout.

The term burnout is familiar to everyone—it comes from the description of a forest after a fire. Before the fire, the forest is alive with promise and beauty, animal and plant life abound, creating its own energy and life. After the fire, the land that once was throbbing with life is now deserted and lifeless with little hope for the future. The same can be said for how we view our work when we become affected by a personal forest fire. In the early stages of burnout, our energy for work becomes depleted. We find ourselves being stressed by even the most simple of tasks. Our motivation and direction become sidelined and we find ourselves in a downward spiral leading to complete exhaustion. Much like the forest after a fire, we have little energy and, for the most part, are lifeless when it comes to our work.

Burnout is more prevalent with individuals but it can also affect businesses and organizations. When an organization becomes affected by burnout everything and everyone in the organization will be impacted. The cost of doing business is negatively impacted as is the bottom line. Employees who experience little job satisfaction become increasingly ineffective affecting the entire operation of the company. The International Labor Organization refers to job burnout as one of the most serious job-related illnesses of the 21st Century. Not only does it affect the health and well-being of the employee, it is estimated that job burnout costs the U.S. economy in excess of $200 billion a year in decreased productivity.

**"Stupidity got us into this mess,
why can't it get us out?"**
—Will Rogers

Many employees can function at a high level of success and still be facing burnout. When this is the case the employee may be masking their burnout by making unhealthy lifestyle choices; including self-destructive behaviors such as alcohol and drug abuse, practicing poor dietary habits or indulging in poor physical or mental activities. Many of these unhealthy life practices are done in an effort to avoid the emotional and physical stress found on their job. Eventually time will catch up with them and the negative life choices they are making may ultimately be more destructive than job burnout. It's simple: if you feel overworked and under-appreciated, it is hard to find the energy needed to be productive.

According to a finding of the Northwest National Life Insurance Company, 'One in four employees identifies work as the number one stressor in his or her life.' St. Paul Fire and Marine Insurance Company identify problems at work as being strongly associated with health complaints and escalating medical cost. Even exceeding the problems associated with family and money concerns. It's not just the physical health of the employees that is affected by burnout; 60% of worker absenteeism results from psychological problems at an estimated annual cost of $57 million. These numbers are supported by the journal of *Occupational Health*, which estimates health cost being 50% higher for workers who report high levels of stress on the job.

The Job is Fun, it's The Work I Hate

That's a lot of statistical jargon and depressing information. But the good news is: laughter can help. By utilizing our sense of humor at work we have a better chance of surviving the 9-5 grind. (The 9-5 grind, now there is a myth!) A good laugh or a change in attitude can help us survive and thrive in today's workplace. Since burnout is the result of workplace stress, humor should help in offsetting burnout by reducing stress. If we can find laughter and incorporate our sense of humor on the job we can develop survival skills that aid in the prevention of burnout.

Every occupation has its own set of stressors. No matter what the job, stress exists. Problems arise when we become preoccupied with outside influences that cause us to lose sight of our own needs. If we lose sight of our needs and fail to recognize our limitations we will start feeling overwhelmed and out of control. When this happens, our productivity drops and we will find ourselves enjoying work less and less.

Should we be worried that doctors call what they do practice?

Most of our adult life will be consumed by work. Since work occupies so much of our life it is imperative that we develop a positive mental attitude toward our work. If we are feeling overwhelmed by negative factors it is difficult to feel good about our hard work. Laughter again can go a long way toward improving our outlook and the environment we work in. When we begin recognizing the humor found in our jobs we will develop a greater ability to deal with the negative factors of our jobs. When we develop this ability we will have more control over our attitude and feelings. A positive attitude can be the fuel for success on the job and in the home.

Hopefully, by discovering laughter and using our sense of humor at work we will become better equipped for the battle against job burnout. Even when things seem to be spinning out of control we always have the ability to take control over our attitude. With the proper attitude we can gain insight and direction as to how we approach work. If we look at our problems on the job as pessimists, we are concentrating on the negative. But if we approach it with an optimistic attitude we may begin to see the challenge as an opportunity. If most of our time is spent complaining and looking on the dark side of situations we are building the foundation for stress and burnout.

We are responsible for our own well-being and we can't depend on others to make us happy—we need to do it for ourselves and this, in many cases, comes down to our attitude and how we look at life and its many situations. By utilizing our sense of humor we not only gain a better handle on our stress we also begin taking control over our attitude. By incorporating laughter into our daily routine the stress of the day will be less powerful and more manageable. When we stop blaming others for our problems and begin taking responsibility for our actions, we can gain greater self-respect and a positive outlook for our work and our situation.

**"I love deadlines. I love the whooshing
sound they make as they fly by."**

—Douglas Adams

One sure way of finding humor at work is to begin viewing daily routines from a comic angle. At the hospital where I worked we collected funny things patents would say. Much like the old Art Linkletter TV show "Kids Say The Darndest Things," we developed our own collection and entitled them: "Alcoholics Say The Darndest Things." We were not trying to be disrespectful to our patients but we were attempting to find humor in our work. If we find time to laugh while on the job we will be able to reduce our stress and increase our productivity. Anyone who works with the public can develop their own collection of funny things people say. It is easy to identify things co-workers or clients say that may be interpreted with a comedic ear. Every day we witness funny things people say and do. All occupations have their share of humor, but if you work with the public you are likely to have an abundance of humor.

*Here are a few of my favorites from
"Alcoholic Say The Darnest Things."*

Once while conducting an admissions interview with an elderly gentleman I came to the following question: *"Prior to your admission to the hospital did you come through detox?"*

Well, he thought and thought repeating several times the word 'detox.' He would press his hand to his forehead indicating his concentration, repeating the word 'detox' when finally he looked up and said, "Well I know we came through Pageland but I don't know about 'Detox.'" Maybe I should have chosen my words a little more carefully but his answer was indeed funny. I had to laugh, and after I chose my words differently, he laughed seeing the humor in his answer. His innocent response provided a nice humor break and the laugher we shared brought us closer together—rather than being a clinician and a client, we became two people sharing a laugh. Not only were we able to share laughter, but I also had a story for my co-workers. Sometimes we fear our laughter may be inappropriate and we are hesitant to demonstrate it. This could have been such a moment but realizing it was an innocent mistake, I didn't hold back my laughter and we both enjoyed the moment.

I had another patient that reported every night she drank herself into "*Bolivia.*" When I asked how she got back it was quickly pointed out it was through "Detox."

One of our patients during his intake reported his occupation as that of a "*migraine worker.*" At first we believed he had misspoken but as we worked with him we soon realized he was indeed a migraine worker. Sometimes the darndest things can be the truest things. The social worker assigned to this gentleman's case reported that he did not suffer from ulcers but was a carrier.

In another incident, a patient did not understand why the hospital was concerned with a country band. This puzzled the staff until we realized he was speaking of the hospital's contraband policy.

A counselor for a social security office reported a man came in to check on his workers' constipation. I know sometimes claims can move slowly but this sounded ridiculous. Every occupation has their own stories: for example, a lady goes to the doctor because of her "very close veins." No matter what the job, you can bet there is humor to be found. You may just need to allow yourself to see it and enjoy it.

Though we are surrounded by humor we only benefit from it when we allow for its enjoyment. I believe that if you suppress laughter when you experience it you may be harming your mind and body. I tell my workshop participants that suppressed laughter goes straight to your hips and you will begin expanding before God and everybody. So let the laughter out and enjoy the moment.

By developing a comic eye like "Candid Camera" or a comic ear like Art Linkletter you will start seeing and hearing the humor that surrounds you. Not only will your attitude improve it may also stimulate some creative thinking. When this takes place our sense of humor and laughter become weapons in the battle of job stress and burnout.

Humor was once dismissed by the professional community as an indication of immaturity. Today's work place has a greater appreciation for wit and a good sense of humor. Both are now considered occupational pluses. A recent survey conducted by Accounttemps of America found that people with a good sense of humor are perceived to be better employees. We enjoy associating with upbeat and optimistic people and if we are using our sense of humor we are demonstrating these positive traits.

Consider your own work environment—who are the coworkers you enjoy being with and around? Most likely the people we enjoy spending time with are the ones who laugh and have a positive view of life. Individuals who laugh and use their sense of humor are perceived to be more relaxed and less confrontational; they add to the workplace rather than detract from it.

A few of the benefits associated with using our humor at work include improved self-confidence, better teamwork and the creation of stronger, supportive relationships. The good feelings that accompany the use of humor will help contribute to a comfortable work environment with increased productivity.

Successful individuals are said to have the ability to impress, influence and lead others. Our sense of humor can be a catalyst for promoting these traits at work or in the community. People like to do business with people they are comfortable with. Dr. Joel Goodman, director of the Sagamore Institute's Humor Project, says that if we have the ability to joke and laugh then we will have the ability to capture others' attention. Goodman says that humor will help in the removal of tension and stress with the added bonus of improved concentration. Humor allows us to grow personally and professionally. Always pack your sense of humor as you climb the ladder of success.

Climb the ladder of success with your sense of humor.

In today's competitive job market a good sense of humor could possibly be what separates candidates for the job. Employers are not only looking for qualified employees but they want employees who possess good communication skills and have the ability to adapt and become productive team members. Employers are looking for individuals who are motivated, creative and can get along well with others. This, in many ways, could be a sub-definition of a good sense of humor and a positive attitude—the ability to get along with others. The use of humor will not only increase our creative thinking but it will also improve our communication skills. Let your sense of humor be a positive part of your professional ability and let it support your resume.

Creative thinking has been the cornerstone for many a successful venture: the Industrial Revolution, the space program—you name it and you can bet it was an outgrowth of creative thinking. So, it is no wonder that employers are beginning to focus on the need for creative thinkers. They are seeking a competitive edge which can be realized by recognizing and encouraging creative thinking. From customer service to the next great invention, creative thinking has been, and will continue to be, at the root of all success.

Laughter can stimulate creative thinking. When we use our senses of humor we are becoming more creative. What makes a joke funny is the incongruity that is presented. This causes the right brain to work and when the right brain begins to work we are thinking creatively. The punch line illustrates the incongruity and delivers the audience to an unexpected conclusion. It is a creative adventure destined for laughter and amusement.

Everyone has heard the catch phrase, "Think outside the box," referring to a situation when a problem is approached from a new or different perspective without traditional restraints. What box are they talking about? How can I think outside the box if I don't recognize the box I'm in? In this case, the box most likely is the one we construct with our thoughts and actions, where we limit ourselves to the safe and comfortable. A great example of in-the-box thinking was that of Charles H. Duell, director of the U.S. Patent Office, who proclaimed in 1899, "Everything that can be invented has been invented," and quit his job. Safe to say he was not a visionary and he did little outside-the-box thinking. Yet he is not alone—so many of us are trapped in self-constructed boxes because the box we construct is considered safe and comfortable.

> *"The crisis of today is the joke of tomorrow."*
> —H. G. Wells

To be outside the box is to venture away from the safe and ordinary. It is not always easy to see situations with a different perspective. But, if we are going to find new solutions, we need to have a creative base for how we think and how we work on our problems. Solutions and ideas spring from creative thinking. Today's workplace calls more and more for creative problem solving—thus, thinking outside the box. Employees today are being asked if there is a better, more efficient way. This is creative thinking moving away from the status quo. Status quo does not always translate into success.

If you do a quick review of the *'Forbes Top 50'* companies listed 25 years ago compared to today's list of the top 50 companies you will discover that many companies did not survive with safe, comfortable thinking. A common trait shared by many successful businesses is the ability to look at challenges from many different perspectives. This outside-the-box thinking allows them to have more control and greater impact on the problems, challenges and situations being faced at work or in the community. One of the biggest benefits of utilizing our senses of humor is that it gives us a base for creative thinking, helping remove us from the traps of the mundane. When we use our senses of humor we are becoming more creative in the way we think and communicate.

Sometimes we need to be creative for unproductive times too. For example, sometimes we may want to call in sick even though we are not really sick. The need for some unauthorized time off is something many of us feel from time to time. In a survey conducted by CareerBuilder.com, more than one third of U.S. workers reported playing hooky from work in the past year. Thirty-five percent of those surveyed reported calling in sick when, in actuality, they felt fine. Even if this is something you have never done, chances are you have considered it. In my workshops I often ask attendee's to take part in a classroom exercise called "Gee Boss." In this exercise, I have participants fill in the reason for not being able to come to work. Using the alphabet as my guide the first excuse will start with the letter A and go on until we have completed the entire alphabet. I jump around the room so participants have no idea when they will be called on for their excuse. The collective response is fun and creative and is always met with laughter and smiles.

The following are some of the excuses that have been offered:

"Gee Boss I can't come to work today because...."

My Alligator ate my car keys.
By Bus changed its route and I ended up at the mall.
My Cat died.
My Door will not open so I can't get out.
My son Eloped.
I just Forgot to come to work.
My pet Goat ate my ID badge.
I Hurt myself getting out of bed.
I have no Idea why I can't come to work.
I'm in Jail.
I'm being held hostage by an angry Kangaroo.
I won the Lottery.
My Monkey stole my car.
I Never liked work anyway.
I am going to be on *Oprah.*
My Pencil broke.
I won the Queen-for-a-Day competition.
I've Run away to join the circus.
I have a Stolen identity.
I Tripped on my dog and I can't get up.
I am Unaware of what I need to do today.
I lost my Voice.
I am going off to War.
My X-Rays show I shouldn't be at work.
Well, You know why I'm not coming in.
My aunt Zelda won the *Price is Right.*

Many successful organizations have a pulse of energy and a supportive nucleus, where everyone is working with the same mission in mind. Shared laughter is one way of getting everyone in the organization to sing from the same hymnal. It's more than sharing a laugh—it's sharing an identity. When we share an identity we will become more respectful and comfortable with each other. When employees are comfortable with each other and they feel support and they are more likely to take on a sense of ownership. When employees feel a sense of ownership they will be more in touch with the needs of the organization and each other, promoting a more productive work environment.

The use of humor can help bring everyone closer together, helping create a positive work environment and productive relationships. An organization that is built on positive relationships and good communication will be better equipped to address its goals and direction. Shared goals are easier to reach, leading to greater success.

More and more, today's successful corporations demonstrate the value of humor and creative thinking and its effects on the bottom line. These organizations see humor as a spirit shot in the arm. Southwest Airlines and Ben & Jerry's Ice Cream are among the companies that have realized the value of laughter and its impact on success. They incorporate humor into the daily operations of their companies—increasing productivity and teamwork, while reducing work related stress. Corporate laughter contributes to an environment of success. Laughter in the workplace can help reduce stressful perceptions while increasing positive feelings, impacting on self-worth and personal responsibility. Everyone in the organization is better served when we realize laughter and fun are resources for success. The overall environment of the organization will lend itself to positive interaction and increased production when humor is a normal asset.

The following humor outlets are suggestions designed to aid in the development of a corporate sense of humor and some creative thinking.

Promoting Humor within an Organization

It's important to recognize the value of creativity in the workforce. A creative work environment not only helps facilitate production and success but also improves morale and communication. Employees should have an outlet for creative thinking and actions. Who is the most qualified to give feedback about the organization and its mission? Employees have firsthand knowledge of what is taking place and their knowledge can be invaluable. Many times valuable information can be gathered through some creative outlets. Also, creative activities can help fight the mundane nature of some jobs. Find ways to promote creative thinking. The following suggestions are designed to help promote creativity and togetherness.

Bumper Sticker Contest

Sponsor a bumper sticker contest. Have participants address the mission of the organization with a bumper sticker. Make each sticker fun and creative. Tell participants to draw on some of their own knowledge of bumper stickers and have fun with it. *"Ask me about our mission statement."; "The sum of all success begins with accounting."; "Customer service begins here."* Award a prize for the most outrageous or creative. Have fun with the idea and post the sticker designs for everyone to see and enjoy. You may be surprised by the information a simple bumper sticker will convey.

Door Decorating Contest

Sponsor a door-decorating contest. Select a theme that everyone can enjoy and then encourage participants to be creative while having fun decorating their office door. If your organization has cubicles, then you can have a 'best cubicle contest' or maybe have teams decorate conference room doors or even bathroom doors. The decorating contest should help individuals take ownership of their workspace, developing a little pride while having fun. If we can identify with something we are more likely to enjoy it and take pride in it. If you are getting ready to enter a stressful time for your organization i.e.: education standardized testing, hospital Joint Accreditation, whatever the reason for the upcoming stress—it can be addressed with a decorative door. This will bring the participants closer together through sharing a common goal, increasing team work and providing a little aversion from stress.

Develop a Joke Book

Ask staff members to share favorite jokes or humorous stories and then assemble them much like you would a cookbook of favorite recipes. Place the collection in a book that everyone has access too. Divide the book into chapters representing different components of your organization. This will not only create a great humor resource but it will also give employees an outlet to demonstrate their senses of humor. One thing that I have learned by collecting humorous stories or jokes is how powerful they are. On those days that are just not going the way you hoped or expected, take a humor break and review the book. A project of this nature will help with morale and bring everyone together.

Write a Group Story

Write an opening paragraph and then have the story written by staff members contributing one paragraph at a time. This will introduce cooperation and creativity. When the story is complete, share it with everyone. It will help promote an environment of laughter and enjoyment. If there are reluctant authors then have them team up to write. The object is not to create stress but to deliver fun and cooperation. Who knows, the next great 'Who done it?' may come out of your office. No matter what, it will be a creative exercise for all to enjoy.

Cartoons on Memos and Emails

Office memos and emails are sometimes lost in translation or lost in the delivery process. These days, very few offices actually use memos since the arrival of email but there was a time when they ruled the roost. When I had to send out memos I often wondered if they were actually being read or if they were just being trashed. Admittedly, the memo does not have as much power as it once did with emails becoming the standard barrier for information. But there are times the memo may still be needed. While working in staff development, I found my memos were not reaching their intended target. I began looking for humorous solutions to the memo challenge. In hopes of finding a way to increase the likelihood of the recipient reading the message, I began placing cartoons on the cover sheet or on the memo itself. The response was terrific! People started reading the message as well as the cartoon and the laughter began. This means of communication became so popular that the staff actually began to look forward to my memos. Laughter can set the stage for communication—so why not try humor on a memo? The same idea can apply to emails. In the subject line put a humorous introduction to get the recipient's attention. Use humor to introduce the email and the subject matter will be covered and read.

Sponsor an Ice Cream Social

Almost everyone loves ice cream. It is hard to look stuffy and aloof when eating a sundae or an ice cream cone. Have team members bring in their favorite flavors and then share. This can help provide a change in attitude and help set the stage for hard work. Sponsor a creative sundae contest or have the staff build their own banana splits. If you are facing a tough week at work diffuse the stress by offering up a little rocky road. The possibilities are endless if you use your imagination and involve some ice cream.

Pot-Luck Lunches

Have employees bring in favorite foods to be shared at a working lunch or a special occasion. This not only promotes team work but it also enables everyone to learn more about special culinary talents co-workers may possess. Possibly do a themed luncheon such as a 'day at the ball park.' Celebrate special days with a special meal. This will not only help build morale, but it will promote teamwork and fun.

Have the supervisory staff prepare a picnic lunch for the rest of the staff, giving everyone an opportunity to see and enjoy others in a different light. Sponsor a chili cook-off in which the staff votes for the best dish. There are so many things that can be done with food as the theme. It's been said that the way to a man's heart is through his stomach, change that a little and you may realize that teamwork can be realized through one's stomach.

Develop a Personalized Organizational Calendar

Develop an organizational calendar that is fun and entertaining. You may take the opportunity to highlight stressful days and occasions that could use a dose of laughter. An organizational calendar can also be used to highlight birthdays and anniversaries as a form of recognition. It's no secret that people enjoy being recognized and what better way to do it than through an organizational calendar? Designate dates for fun activities and special events. It's your calendar—let it reflect your organization. If you feel really creative include weekly ideas for success on the calendar such as, 'Don't be caught at the airport when your ship comes in,' or 'An apple a day keeps the doctor away but an onion a day will keep everyone away.'

Open Staff Meetings with Humor

Opening staff meetings with a humorous anecdote or joke can promote some laughter, and with laughter, comes relaxation. The ensuing laughter helps put staff members at ease resulting in reduced tension. The humorous story helps create a positive environment for a productive meeting. Many of us are in agreement with Milton Berle who said, "Meetings are where we create minutes by wasting hours." So begin the meeting with some humor and strive to share some fun.

**"Meetings are where we create minutes
by wasting hours."**
—Milton Berle

The reason most after-dinner speakers begin their presentation with a humorous anecdote is simple—they are trying to connect with the audience by increasing everyone's comfort level. When holding a staff meeting, the need should be the same. We want to make a connection and set the participants at ease for a productive meeting. Using humor in this manor helps create a stronger bond for those attending. Shared laughter goes a long way in helping individuals and organizations overcome negative thoughts while creating a positive, productive environment.

At some point in my career I have used all of the previous suggestions with positive results. The key benefit of these exercises was improved morale and increased productivity. If we can share a laugh then we can share a goal.

Chapter 8

Laughter: It's a Family Affair

If laughter is good for the individual then you know it's going to be great for the family. Families will endure joyous times and stressful times and a dose of humor will benefit both. With laughter comes the ability to see ourselves in an honest, reflective light. Not only will laughter strengthen our relationships—it can also create an emotional bridge for togetherness. Everyone in the family can benefit from a good laugh making it truly a great medicine that all can enjoy.

No matter what role we have within our family it will continually evolve. From birth to the grave our role is ever-changing. It may even change from day to day or even from hour to hour. I am a son, a father, a brother, a husband, an uncle, a cousin and a nephew. Our interactions are defined by the role we find ourselves in.

Family dynamics will always have an impact on our role and how we use our humor. My mother still refers to me as the baby of the family. Well into my 50's, I am not nearly as put off by this statement as I used to be. Today the Baby Boomer generation is becoming known as the "Sandwich Generation" with parents needing care as well as children. It is easy to become overwhelmed by the roles we find ourselves in if we fail to keep a proper perspective on them. Failure to keep things in perspective will produce stress and tension which have the potential to erode the nucleus of a strong family.

**"Santa Claus has the right idea…
Visit people only once a year."**

—Victor Borge

No matter what role you find yourself in, a constant will always be the need for laughter. Laughter can bring balance and objectivity to family dynamics. Laughter can help create a realistic view of life and the challenges families face. It is important to ensure your family tree has some roots based in laughter.

Unfortunately the old saying, "Every silver lining has a dark cloud," may apply to many families as well. Regrettably, every family will at some point experience negative emotions. When negative dynamics are present they usually are accompanied by the production of an array of unhealthy emotions and actions. If left unchecked, negative emotions will only grow and fester having the potential to harm everyone. One way of off-setting negative emotions is to try to discover some joy no matter what your role is at the time.

When you allow yourself to enjoy humor and laughter you will discover an improved attitude toward your life and family. Families that share laughter will enjoy stronger and more appropriate relations. Of course, our laughter should be respectful and fun—not hurtful and inappropriate. Inappropriate humor has the potential to divide a family. Laugh with one another and not at each other. When laughter becomes a positive resource for the family everyone will develop stronger bonds and improved relationships.

Actually, family hierarchies vary little from places of employment. Usually parents take on the role of management and children take the role of employees. (Well, this may be a stretch… or just wishful thinking.) The roles we assume in our family interactions can either contribute to or negate positive relationships. Just as in an organization or place of business, families can improve their togetherness and strengthen their relationships by discovering and utilizing their humor. It is important to set the stage for the use and development of our sense of humor. It's not a stretch to say, "A family that laughs together stays together."

Shared laughter not only helps families reaffirm each other's love, but it helps bring them closer. Family laughter will enhance everyone's sense of belonging. When we cultivate our humor as a family we are learning and demonstrating strategies that can help dispel anger and aggression while promoting togetherness. Humor, when used appropriately, helps everyone grow and survive. When a family shares a smile or a laugh, good things happen. This is especially true during hard times. Laughter is a tool that all families can use to help find the strength needed when dealing with negative events.

As I wrestle with my mother's declining health. I will often think about her wonderful sense of humor and how she would encourage us to laugh every day. She not only set the stage for laughter, she promoted it. From her I learned that no matter what the situation, a little smile goes a long way. Mom always demonstrated her love for life with laugher. I have always respected my mother's humor and now I recognize that her wiliness to laugh not only touched my life, but the lives of everyone she came into contact with.

A family that laughs together stays together.

All families should strive to share laughter. It should be viewed as an essential ingredient for a successful, happy family. Everyone in the family should share humor; it opens communications, increases togetherness and it is just plain fun. Children can provide countless hours of humor for their parents and, in turn, parents should contribute to the laughter of their children. Learning the value of laughter can be a life lesson the entire family can share.

In today's fast pace world it's not unusual for parents to feel the stress of parenting sometimes brought on by over-scheduling a child's time. If a child's time is over-scheduled then the parent is over-scheduled. Well-meaning parents trying to give their children ample opportunities fall victim to scheduling nightmares. If your child needs to be at soccer practice, take a piano lesson, go to dance and attend gymnastics all at the same time, then you better have a sense of humor. Without a sense of humor the stress and tension will increase to the point that everyone in the family will become victims of burnout. Hopefully this scenario is an exaggeration, but too often it is closer to reality than it should be.

When over-scheduling takes place, most parents will begin to feel stress, and when the parent feels stress the child will too. In many households, the saying, "If Mama ain't happy nobody's happy," is posted for everyone to see. Many can identify with this statement. When someone in the household is not happy their disposition and unhappy attitude can affect everyone in the household. Of course you may wish to change this to say, "If Mama is stressed then the family is stressed." When we find ourselves over-stressed we are less likely to enjoy the very things that were designed to be fun and entertaining.

It's during these times that a good dose of humor can not only help relieve the stress but can also help put things back into a proper perspective. By recognizing what contributes to our discomfort we gain greater control over what actions we should take to care for ourselves. Maybe it's time to slow down and give the children a chance to be children and the parents a chance to be more than a taxi service. In slowing down you may find you enjoy yourself and family more.

Children who develop the ability to share laughter possess greater coping skills and develop a more positive self-image. Children may not understand the physical and mental advantages of laughter—these benefits can be learned later. The important thing is that parents strive to create and facilitate laughter with the entire family. A child that enjoys laughter and humor will develop a positive outlook on life and have greater defenses in the constant battle against stress and negative emotions. If we can promote laughter with children they will be less likely to feel frustrated and anxious when things don't go as planned.

Children will experience the same emotions as adults. This includes joy and happiness, but they will also experience frustrations, anger and sadness. The beauty of laughter is that it is a simple resource that is available to everyone—adults and children alike. Children are no different than adults; if they can find something to laugh about, they too feel less vulnerable and out of control. If we teach our children the value of a good positive laugh they will benefit from it for years to come. Children who enjoy laughter seem to have an innate ability to bounce back from disappointment quicker. In life, laughter goes a long way for kids and adults.

We all experience disappointment but the ability to draw on our sense of humor enables us to handle our disappointment and setbacks more effectively. I was able to learn this lesson early on by watching the little leaguers I coached. All coaches want to succeed but when you are dealing with children, success should be measured in different ways. Unfortunately, if success is measured by wins and losses it comes at a cost. On the ball field, someone's success is always accompanied with someone's disappointment. All it took for me to get over the disappointment of a loss was to see the kids playing after the game. Sure, the loss was disappointing to them, but most of them didn't let disappointment ruin their day. You soon realize children who laugh and play have the ability to process disappointment more effectively. When I saw my team begin playing and joking around with each other I realized they had put the disappointing loss behind them and so should I.

Everyone one can learn a great deal from the laughter of a child and a child's perspective. The cynic in all of us would say children fail to see the full picture in many circumstances. They don't know enough about the situation to understand the disappointment, allowing them to accept what they have little understanding or control over. If that's the case, then maybe timing is everything and this is another lesson we can learn from children—things happen and life goes on. We should not let our disappointment hinder our recovery. We need to allow our senses of humor to become a healing factor in our struggles to overcome disappointment.

"Childhood is a time of rapid changes. Between the ages of 12 and 17 a parent can age 30 years."

—Sam Levenson

Many times children have the ability to see humor in a situation when adults fail to. A favorite childhood memory of mine demonstrates this perfectly. My father and my uncle Mamers (Yes that was his real name. He was named for a small town in NC. You see, humor came naturally in our family.) were celebrating the fact they were on vacation. Unfortunately, their celebration lasted well into the night. Their celebration lasted much longer than my mother and aunt had wished. My father, home on leave from the Air Force, and uncle Mamers, a railroad man, were enjoying the first day of a two-week vacation. After enjoying more than their fair share of adult beverages, they sat in matching rocking chairs and began toasting the coming vacation days. When not conducting their toasts, they sang the hits of the day, all the while telling stories of the wonderful things they would accomplish while on vacation. Neither was feeling any pain. Rest assured, they were going to feel the pain the next morning, but on this night they were happy being away from work and just thinking about their time off.

My mother and aunt were not very happy with their husbands and their frustration seemed to grow with every song the two men sang. Neither my mother nor her sister could see any humor in what was going on. After all, they too were on vacation and this was not the way they had envisioned it starting. All of us kids not only thought it was funny but we saw little reason for concern. I still remember my uncle rocking in his chair between choruses of "Ole Shep" saying, "Thirteen glorious days! Thirteen glorious days!" referring to how many more vacation days he had left. Now close to 50 years later I still laugh about that night. Of course I do have an appreciation for the stress my mother and her sister must have felt, but that doesn't erase the smile from my face.

An apple a day keeps the doctor away but a laugh a day keeps families together.

Today, whenever Barry or I bring up that night to our mother she will smile and laugh, usually saying something derogatory under her breath, but laughing all the while. This is the power of humor. If we can remove ourselves from the event we can usually find humor in it. Remember, a spoonful of sugar and a spoonful of humor may work in the same way. It gives us the power to accept and deal with troubling times with a little more ease. Acceptance gives us a measure of control and with control comes the ability to adjust our attitude and our feelings.

Watch a child at play and you will begin to understand how children seem to realize that a key to an enjoyable life is laughter. Unfortunately, this insightful behavior is generally lost in childhood. Too often children will begin losing their sense of humor early on because of the maturing process. Children are being programmed not to use humor. No matter if it is intentional or not, the results are the same: our children too often lose the joy. (*How many times have you heard a parent say, "Wipe that smile off your face," or ask "What's so funny?"),* When you grow up hearing these statements you get the impression that humor and laughter are not important and may actually be perceived as bad traits. Parents should strive to put a smile on the faces of their children and while doing so have one on their faces as well.

Children are not immune to feelings that are considered to be adult feelings. They will feel anger, frustration or stress and, if these emotions are not addressed, just as with an adult the child's psyche can be adversely affected. This makes it important for parents to encourage their children to laugh and to use their sense of humor. The stressors children face may be different from their parents but to a child the stress can be every bit as real. Failure to deal with the stress can lead to physical and emotional problems.

Parents can have a positive affect on a child's humor development by supporting the use of laughter. They should also encourage the child to share laughter and see humor in the world. When children are exposed to laughter they will become more relaxed and will enjoy greater social advantages when dealing with people outside the home.

Parents can influence their children's humor by selecting movies, books or stories that can be shared with the entire family. Children can see the true advantage of humor when they witness their parents enjoying it. The demonstration and encouragement of laughter helps create unity. Humor can help knock down walls of anger, alienation, and frustration. A little laughter can go a long way.

> ### *"Parents are the last people on earth who should have children."*
>
> *—Samuel Butler*

Families present great opportunities for laughter. Unfortunately, many families allow outside influences to block laughter. This occurs when families allow stress and negative emotions to enter into their relationships. It may be as simple as slowing down and taking time to recognize the humor we all live with. As we recognize the humor that surrounds us, the next step is to lighten up our attitude and have a good laugh. Share a smile and good things will happen. Open your eyes, ears and heart to those you love and you can't help but see the humor. Not only will we benefit from the laughter, our friends and loved ones will benefit as well.

Another important thing is to laugh at yourself—especially if you are a parent. When we laugh at ourselves we are actually helping our children learn a valuable lesson in life. When you can laugh at yourself you hold the power to conquer many obstacles in life. If we can laugh at our mistakes, the mistakes may still be embarrassing but we will find our laughter gives us some measure of control over the events. What is the worst thing that can happen? A little self-deprecation can go a long way. This is an area where parents can instill the value of laughter by demonstrating that no matter how embarrassing or stressful an event may be—it can be handled with a chuckle or smile.

Parents will often try to use humor to change a child's focus or redirect a child's energy from a negative event. My parents did it, I've done it and you probably have as well. Humor helps change the focus from a bruised arm or a scraped knee. My parents had a standard line when either my brother or I suffered a small scrape or bruise; I must have heard it a 100 times: *"It will be all right before you get married"*. This observation didn't do much for my pain but more than once it did bring a smile to my face. Not only did this lame statement change my mindset, it also demonstrated that if they were not too worried about the injury then and I was probably overreacting anyway. They were helping me realize that my minor injury was just that—minor. It wasn't going to be with me for long. The line I use for my children is, *"Just rubbed some dirt on it and you will be fine."* Fortunately my children have been smart enough not to heed my advice. Most of the time, they would see the absurdity of the statement and begin to laugh or at least give me one of those looks that said what I could do with my dirt theory. Their eyes would say, "That's not funny, Dad,"; but they would be less preoccupied with the mishap. A little engaged laughter helps everyone to reduce fear and lessen stress while promoting goodwill.

The quality of any relationship can be judged by the presence of humor. It seems everyone wants to find a partner with a good sense of humor. No matter if it's the first date or the 30th wedding anniversary, the more couples appreciate each other's sense of humor the more satisfaction they will experience in the relationship. A healthy, strong relationship will always have laughter. All relationships benefit from humor but it is especially true when it comes to our families and spouses. Families that enjoy laughter have a strong foundation for lasting relationships. A key benefit to a shared laugh is improved communications and the development of a stronger bond between family members.

> **"When I was kidnapped, my parents snapped into action. They rented out my room."**
> **—Woody Allen**

Though everyone is born with the ability to laugh, the development of our sense of humor is largely a byproduct of the company we keep. Children will genuinely begin the development of their sense of humor in the second year of life. It is during this year that they begin engaging in fantasy or make-believe. The parent can positively impact the child's humor by supporting their creative spirit and use of humor. Think about your own childhood. Was laughter shared and encouraged? If it was then you most likely have a good sense of humor today. If, however, you grew up in a strict, humorless household then you may have trouble relating to humor and its importance. If this is the case you may need to do some work cultivating your sense of humor. The benefits will be well worth it. Remember: sharing laughter opens doors and improves attitudes. Laughter in a relationship is always a win-win.

People are attracted to each other for any number of reasons. But what most likely cements a strong, lasting relationship is the ability to get along. Laughter is a key ingredient to getting along. It's difficult to remain angry at each other when you could share a laugh instead. Laughter brings people together and this is especially true for couples. Couples that share laughter generally enjoy good communication and with good communication comes increased respect and consideration—all key components in a quality relationship. Divorce attorneys identify the number one reason for divorce as that of irreconcilable differences—couples are just not getting along. Maybe there are several reasons couples fall out of love, but you can bet if they are not getting along then they are not sharing laughter. When we don't have the energy for laughter in our relationships they become dull and uneventful. This can lead to possible breakups or at least to unhappy or unfulfilling relationships.

It's simple: a family that shares laughter will have a greater chance of survival and happiness. With 50% of marriages ending in divorce, it's easy to see the importance of sharing something everyone can enjoy. Why not make it a laugh?

Families that enjoy traditions or regular activities—vacations, birthday parties, ect.—have a stronger sense of togetherness. Traditions can be enhanced with shared laughter. Enjoying a tradition as a family creates a sense of pride and togetherness. Whether it's having dinner together, playing a board game or watching a favorite TV show, the important thing is that the family is doing it together.

I have a close friend whose family exercises their humor weekly. Once a week they have a humor dinner smorgasbord. The rules are simple: before gathering for dinner each family member has to find something humorous to bring to the table. It can range from a joke to a humorous story or maybe something found in a paper or magazine. It makes no difference as long as the presenter finds some humor in it. Following the meal they will present their finding. The anticipation of what will be shared at the table makes the meal itself a humorous event. Everyone dining that night is asked to share; if they have a guest for dinner on these nights, well, they are expected to share a laugh as well.

The beauty of these dinners is that they give everyone the opportunity to demonstrate their sense of humor and experience laughter. My friend echoes the philosophy that a family that laughs together stays together. A stronger bond is developing with a little humor and a comedic eye. Good feelings are shared by all. A byproduct of these humor dinners is how it positively affected the children's self-esteem. When a child learns the value of laughter in a supportive environment they are developing a wonderful resource for life. My friend says the dinners have always been fun, not necessarily funny, but fun just the same. At first, it created some stress on the family but once they started sharing and laughing they grew closer as a family and even began looking forward to the smorgasbord of humor. Personally, I feel he should write a book titled *"Humor at the Dinner Table: A Tale of a Humorous Family."*

My children have always provided me with laughter. My son Andrew is an analytical thinker. When he was six-years-old he came up with some off-the-wall ideas. So many, in fact, that I have my own collection that I call, "Wisdom of a six-year old."

On one occasion while taking him to school he announced that he knew what to do about the world's hunger problem. When I heard he had a solution to the world hunger problem I was immediately impressed. Not only did my six-year-old son realize there was a world hunger problem, but he knew what to do about it.

Of course I had to ask, *"What would you do about the world hunger problem?"*

He simply replied, *'Build more restaurants.'*

Why didn't I think of that? I'm not sure what this said of our eating habits but he indeed had a solution.

Once on a trip to visit my mother in North Carolina we traveled by the NC Motor Speedway a race track that has featured NASCAR racing for many years. We passed it on race day and Andrew was very interested in the race and the fast driving. After some discussion he reasoned that if they started the races earlier in the day they wouldn't have to drive so fast. Now that's logic you can't argue with.

My daughter Lila, who is an animal lover, announced when she was five that she wanted to be vegetarian when she grew up. This surprised everyone but I soon learned that what she meant to say was that she wanted to a veterinarian not a vegetarian. She is often playing veterinarian with her friends. One day I discovered several pieces of paper that listed her stuffed animal as the patient, the problem and what needed to be done. These pieces of paper are priceless. On the following page are some examples (the spelling has not been changed):

Name Prinsess
Date 3-3
Time 4:11
Owners name: Hanna
Whats wrong – Broken Tail
What we do? CAST

Name Scmago
Date 3-3
Time 4:14
Owner becca
What's wrong Can't talk
What wedo? Can talk

Name Big Ears
Date 3-3
Time 3:53
Owners name: Hannah
What's wrong? Wood in foot
What we do? Poled it out/cut open
/stickers and cast

It was a busy day at the Lila Patterson Animal clinic. No matter what the complaint it seemed most of the animals received a cast. Creativity and fun for the kids and a lot of laughter for a Dad.

By the time you make ends meet you discover they moved the ends.

These ailments made me laugh and I also appreciated the creativity that went into it. I keep these papers in my desk and I refer back to them for a smile. Once again a demonstration of how the creativity of a child can produce a laugh.

Once while playing school my daughter drew up the following hall pass.

Nurse Pass

Bleting   teacher_____
Throwing Up   Name _____
Bludy nose
Crying   Other

(In the interest of humor the spelling has not been changed.) I really like the Bludy nose (Bloody Nose) and the Bleting (Bleeding). Children are a great source of humor.

My oldest son Zach at the age of four while on vacation begged us to let him ride "the alligator." We didn't need to be concerned because "the alligator" he was speaking of was in actuality "the elevator. "

Another favorite memory of Zach's childhood was when he would return after visiting my parents for a week. He would come home with all types of stories—many of which I had heard as a young boy myself. During these visits he was able to learn firsthand the roots of his sense of humor. He still claims these were some of the most enjoyable times of his childhood.

I have a stepson who is multi-handicapped and has special needs. But this doesn't keep him from making everyone laugh. He is always smiling and shows a love of life that everyone could learn from. Though he has disabilities he has an infectious laugh that affects everyone he comes into contact with. One year in school he was placed in a Spanish class. He really didn't understand why the teachers were speaking a language he didn't recognize. His short stay in this class led to a favorite line of ours—the teachers said he would become upset and yell, "No buenos dias."

He loves all types of music but his favorite is country. This leads him to quote lines from his favorite songs. When we go out to eat you can bet he will call the waitress a "red neck woman." No one is safe from his use of country music.

My older boys still provide me with a great deal of humor either on the phone or on a visit. I am very close to them and I contribute some of that closeness to the fact that we share laughter. Both are willing participants when it comes to using humor.

All parents can see humor in their children and, rest assured, children see humor in their parents. I often think about my father's humor and how he used it in raising Barry and I. During the second semester of college, I took a chemistry course, or maybe I should say a chemistry course took me. In other words,

I was not doing particularly well in the class and this resulted in my trying to explain my failing mark to my parents. My father said that I was the only one he knew who took pride in making a "high F." It was still an F but I told him it was indeed a "high F." His point: Don't be proud of failure. Work hard, improve and find real pride in success.

Celibacy is not hereditary.

My father was able to draw on his sense of humor to make a point and when he did, it was hard to argue with his logic. After all, his humor had served him well. He grew up in the Depression, joined the service, fought in two wars and raised two children. His humor may have been put to the test but it remained an important part of his life and it was a gift he gave to all of us.

As a child I failed to appreciate his humor as much as I should have. I guess I thought everyone's dad had this quality. But as I entered the real world, I realized just how special his humor was and what it meant to our entire family. My father had the ability to make a point while using his sense of humor helping diffuse potential problems. Of course, there were those times that this tactic just made you mad but I soon learned it was easier to laugh than to sulk.

One of my favorite memories of my father's use of humor concerns my brother Barry. During Barry's senior year in high school, he had lobbied to attend a Four Season's concert in Raleigh NC. We lived about 40 miles outside of Raleigh and if Barry did go, he would be out later than usual and would have to take the car out of town. Barry felt he could plead his case more successfully if he appealed to my father's youthful memories. Barry compared his going to Raleigh to see the Four Seasons to Dad going to see Harry James in his youth.

To this my father replied, "Son, I wouldn't walk across the street to watch a gnat eat a bale of hay much less go to Raleigh to see Harry James."

My brother was left with no argument and when he finally stopped laughing at the thought of a gnat eating a bale of hay all he could do was say that he believed he would have to cross the street to see that. My father used his humor to take control of the conversation and make his point without confrontation or anger. In the end, I am pretty sure that Barry got to go to the concert but we are still looking for a gnat with a giant appetite.

Before the start of my freshman year in college, I really learned the power of my father's humor and wit. He was the victim of a violent crime and was robbed and shot in the leg at close range. This was a traumatic event for everyone, but it was through the strength of my father's humor that we were able to deal with the tragedy successfully. While being admitted to the hospital after losing a great amount of blood, he maintained his humor. The attending physician asked my father if he had any allergies. Daddy told the doctor that he must be allergic to chewing gum. This was a puzzling answer so the physician asked why my father felt he was allergic to chewing gum. My father explained that he feared gum because he had an uncle who lived to be a 103. His uncle never drank or smoked, so he figured it was the chewing gum that did him in. When the doctor told my mother this story she knew he was already on the road to recovery.

Knowing my father was able to use his sense of humor following such a tragic event was a valuable lesson for the entire family. His humor became a bridge to recovery and it was a bridge the entire family could use. We all feared the worst but through a simple laugh we were able to face the tragedy with some reassurance given to us by my father's use of humor. Once we learned how he was using his sense of humor we realized we should follow his lead and begin to find something to laugh about as well.

While in the hospital recovering from the gun shot Dad once again used his humor to give my brother some insight into making life decisions. Barry had recently graduated from college and was about to enter the service. Dad suggested that he look into becoming a helicopter pilot. Well, this was at the height of the Vietnam War and the reported life expectancy for helicopter pilots was somewhat low. After voicing his concern to my father, Dad responded by telling Barry that he was a tail gunner in World War II and their life expectancy was somewhat short as well. He told Barry that though the life expectancy was low he had made it back to Harnett County before he got shot, some 25 years later. He was demonstrating his humor while making a valid statement. His response, though humorous, indicated to Barry that he needed to make his own decision. After all, in life there are no guarantees.

We all learned from Dad by the way he used his sense of humor to help him survive some difficult times. As a parent I have tried to demonstrate what my father taught me about the importance of a good laugh and an active sense of humor. One of the greatest lessons he taught me was that there is always time to laugh.

I have a friend who is a Baptist minister and when called on to conduct a funeral he will ask the family if they remember a favorite joke or a humorous story of the deceased. This gets the family thinking more about how the deceased lived and less about how they died. He will then ask if he could share the story in the service. He has discovered that when asked to remember a loved one's humor, the families quickly begin recounting humorous times and soon their tears are replaced with smiles. When we remember the quality of one's life and reflect on the positive times, we have a greater capacity to accept their passing. When he shares the story in the service he is giving everyone an opportunity to remember the deceased as they lived and a chance to celebrate his or her life.

All families can benefit from sharing laughter. The resources for humor are endless and the benefits will last a lifetime. Families that share laughter have a greater sense of support and belonging. Shared laughter helps everyone develop the strength to handle the bad times and enjoy the good times. Families that fail to share laughter are more likely to be distant and cold, missing out on some wonderful times and memories.

"I have found that the best way to give advice to your children is to find out what they want and then advise them to do it."

—Harry Truman

Many times it only takes a quick look in the mirror to discover some humor. Sometimes the best meaning parents will say some very funny things. When traveling with kids that are acting out in the backseat you may find yourself asking, *"Do you want me to come back there?"* Sure, you're driving 55 miles an hour and threatening to get in the backseat! I'm surprised my children didn't say, "Sure dad, come on back," just to agitate me more.

Then there are those times that our children fail to listen and what do we ask: "How many times do I have to tell you?" As if they were going to answer, "Let's see, this is the fifth time you've asked so I think I should have it down soon—keep asking." Have you ever sent your child to his or her room with the instructions: "Don't come out until you know how to act"? Are we expecting them to emerge from the room quoting Shakespeare: "To be or not to be"? It may be true that kids say the darndest things but they are not alone. Parents have a tendency to say some funny things as well.

The health of a family can be measured and enhanced by the number of shared laughs. Discover your family's humor and begin enjoying it.

Chapter 9

You've Got to be Joking

Someone once said that when you laugh the whole world will laugh with you. But mess up a joke and the whole world will laugh at you. Many attempts at telling jokes have failed due to poor execution or timing. A fumbled punchline can leave everyone wondering what happened... Did I miss something? Was I supposed to have laughed? In the 80's, *Wendy's* restaurants had a tagline for their advertisements that asked "Where's the Beef?" When we are telling jokes we really don't want to hear "Where's the humor?" Mark Twain said the study of humor was like dissecting a frog. When you dissect a frog you can learn a lot about the frog, but, unfortunately, the frog dies. Mark Twain believed studying humor could end up in the death of humor. Let's hope that's not the case. Instead let's try to gain a little insight into the art of joke telling and maybe this will help us in our efforts.

Our sense of humor relates to how we process humor. And joke telling is an acquired art. Okay, maybe it is not an art but it certainly is a skill and every skill requires a little work to develop and improve. So the ability to be a successful joke teller may take a little work.

Everyone enjoys a good joke and we can find even greater joy if we learn how to tell them. The ability to tell jokes improves our communication skills and may even help in breaking down barriers or increasing togetherness. One of the main benefits of learning to tell jokes correctly is the impact it can have on you and your audience. If we can successfully tell a joke then we can successfully communicate with others. Joke telling can be a wonderful tool for sharing and communicating humor. A little wit can go a long way in life. Whether you're at a party or attending a board meeting, utilizing your sense of humor can be instrumental in how well you get along with co-workers and friends. It can also be a factor in your personal and professional success.

I have addressed the positive effects of humor showing how laughter can be a major indicator of a positive workplace and a healthy home. Shared laughter helps set the stage for good communication and positive relationships. These reasons and many more make it important to learn to communicate humor. The ability to share humor can help open doors for positive communication and growth.

Energizer bunny arrested on battery charges.

If you are uncomfortable in telling a joke their probably is a reason. Maybe you have trouble remembering the joke or you just fear failure. Some people are hesitant to share a joke out of fear that their audience has already heard it. This reminds me of an old *New Yorker* cartoon that featured a man with a smoking gun standing over a man who had just been shot. Looking at the police officer, the man with the gun says, "He said to stop him if I had heard it before." So, even if they have heard it before, then what's the worst that can happen? My rule of joke telling is simple: take a chance. If I liked it there is a good possibility that someone else will as well.

A key to a successful joke is to take ownership of the delivery, do it in a fashion that reflects who you are and hope for the best. There is an old story about a man who has been sentenced to prison and is looking for a way to make an impression on his fellow inmates. He thinks he has found just the way when he learns how the inmates tell jokes to one another. While he sits in his cell he hears inmates yell out numbers. After each number is called out the cell block usually breaks out in laughter. He is intrigued so he asks his cell mate what is going on with the numbers and why everyone is laughing. His cell mate explains that most of the inmates have been in the prison so long that everyone has heard the same jokes over and over again. So, rather than tell the entire joke they have numbered them allowing for them to just scream out a number. This saves time and gets the joke told. The new prisoner recognized that joke number 17 seemed very popular. Every time someone yelled "17," the cell block would burst out laughing. So he decides to yell out "17" the next night hoping for an in with his fellow inmates.

The next night when everyone was quiet he screamed out "17." To his horror nobody laughed. He is puzzled. He asks his cellmate, "What went wrong?"

"I choose one of the most popular jokes, and still no one laughed."

His cell mate replies, "Some people can tell a joke and some can't."

If this sounds familiar and you can relate to the story, you are not alone. One thing to remember is that not all jokes need to be fresh and new. The key is to tell the joke in a fresh fashion. If Adam were to return to earth the only thing he would recognize would be the jokes. Everyone has a favorite song and they don't mind hearing it over and over again. As a matter of fact, it is the repetition of the song that made it so popular in the first place. Top 40 radio stations play the same block of songs regularly. So why should we fear hearing the same joke over again? If it makes you smile there is a good bet it will make others smile too.

**Borrow money from a pessimist,
they don't expect it back.**

The real treasure in telling a joke is how it stimulates laughter for the listener as well as the one telling it. We were taught at an early age that it is better to give than to receive—so begin sharing your humor and watch the laughter start.

As with any talent it takes some practice to master. If we can get to the point when we enjoy telling jokes and funny stories then our family and friends will enjoy them as well. The following are some suggestions aimed to help learn the art of telling jokes and the ability to remember them.

Why is it that the people who are great at remembering jokes can't remember how many times they have already told it to you?

Practice, Practice, Practice

If your discomfort for telling a joke comes from a fear that you will not tell the joke correctly, then you may need a little practice. This discomfort in many cases reflects a lack of confidence. It may take practice to change your comfort level. To practice your joke-telling skills, begin slowly and work on delivery and content. Identify jokes that you like, write them down and put them to memory. With the joke written out you can practice your delivery without worrying about content. At first, read the joke aloud. Do this in front of the mirror paying attention to your body language and energy. I know this may seem a little ridiculous but it will pay off in the end. Once you put the joke to memory and have practiced telling it several times you're ready begin telling it to others.

First you may want to practice with family members or close friends. Tell them you heard a joke recently and that you want to try it out on them. If you haven't been known for telling jokes, your friends may be a little surprised—but they will want to be supportive. Remember almost everyone loves a good joke. By practicing with a supportive audience you lower the chances of embarrassment. As with any skill, the more you practice the better the results.

A bird in your hand is safer than one over your head.

With time your comfort level and ability will improve and you will be on your way to being a sharer of wit. Like practicing a speech in the mirror you can work on your delivery and mannerisms as well as develop your animation. The rewards will be worth the work.

Keep a joke journal

A leading reason for not telling a joke is, "I just can't remember them." Don't let this be your excuse. When you hear a joke you enjoy, write it down and put it in your collection. Writing down the joke helps in two ways: first off, it is easier to remember, and second, it increases your humor resources. If you are unable to capture the entire joke, write down the punch line and hopefully when you refer back to the punch line you will be able to recall the whole story.

Few women admit their age; few men act theirs.

Remembering jokes can become a great source for fun and entertainment. When we get into the habit of writing down jokes we will be more likely to share them. As your humor resources grow so does your use of humor. You will soon discover your own style that hopefully everyone will enjoy.

Know when to tell a joke

Knowing when to tell a joke is crucial to how others will appreciate it. Before you set out to tell a joke, check your audience. It's important to take into account what the atmosphere is or what may be happening at the time. Always consider whether a joke could improve the situation or be beneficial for the listeners. In the right situation, a joke can help everyone relax. But, in the wrong situation or at an inappropriate time, no matter how well the joke is told it will still be met with resistance. Don't waste a good joke with bad timing. Know your audience and know the environment before you tell it. A good joke at the right time will help reduce stress and strengthen relationships; At the wrong time, it may just be a waste of breath. Telling a joke is much like performing a rain dance—timing is everything.

Try to relate the joke to the environment

It becomes easier to identify the humor in a situation if we can relate to it. Draw on your environment to make the joke personal and your audience will appreciate it more. You can do this by putting people and things you know in the joke. When we personalize a joke we help our listeners identify and relate to the story. The listeners become more engaged when the joke is personalized. Bridging the gap between the listener and the one telling the joke will results in greater success and enjoyment.

Use sounds and dialects in telling the joke

Don't be afraid to spice up the story with a few sound effects or a change in dialect. This is a good way to poke fun at yourself. Sound effects can add energy and definition to the story. By using creative sounds and dialects, you will find your audience becomes more appreciative and will respect your personal investment. Strive to create a strong visual in the listener's mind. Use descriptive and colorful words to help bring the joke to life.

Use real life observations

By using real life observations you can add realism and interest to the story. Similar to drawing on our environment for humor, real life observations in our jokes create a grateful and engaged listener. Everything in life is more enjoyable when we can relate to it. Don't be afraid to laugh at your world. Take time to find humor in the world around you and then begin sharing it with others.

Engage the listeners

Always engage your audience. As the storyteller you may feed off the listener's energy and interest. This allows the listener to become a bigger part of the story producing greater enjoyment. An invested listener is a good listener. Engaged listeners are always the best—seek to bring them into the story. When this is the case, everyone wins.

React to your own jokes

Your energy level will reflect your commitment. The energy you use gives the joke life and style. Show appreciation for your own jokes. If you don't laugh at the joke then why should anyone else? Your own appreciation for the joke will help everyone appreciate it more. In a sense, you are inviting your listeners to laugh and enjoy the joke with you.

Become animated

Become animated with the story by using body motions and facial expressions. If your body shows you are enjoying the experience, you will have greater success. Take a few cues from your favorite comedian. Notice how he or she uses facial and body movements. Animation will enhance the joke. Again, this allows the audience to use more than their auditory skills—the story becomes more visual. Visualize yourself on a stage and enjoy it. A little animation can add to the fun and the joke will be better received.

Don't find humor at the expense of others

If someone slips on a banana peel, that's an accident. But if you slip on a banana peel, then it's funny. Know when to laugh. Finding humor in the misfortune of others should not be a resource for laughter. Laughter can be a wonderful tool for communication and for positive feelings, but when it is the result of someone else's misfortune it becomes cruel and hurtful. There is enough humor in the world without taking advantage of the less fortunate. Your sense of humor is a valuable resource and should be used productively not to the detriment of others. Laugh at yourself and laugh with others—just try not to laugh *at* others.

Humor like History Repeats Itself

Things to avoid in telling a joke

Don't tell a joke you are not comfortable with. Your discomfort will show and if you are uncomfortable your audience will pick up on it. If you are not sure how to tell the joke then save it for another time. Humor is timeless and can always be used later. If others fail to see the humor in your joke, don't apologize. Don't make excuses for lack of laughter. You tried and maybe next time the laughter will come. The key is to continue having fun telling your jokes.

Chapter 10

Cultivating your Sense of Humor

The following suggestions are offered to help in the identification of and use of your sense of humor. Earlier chapters covered the many physical and mental benefits of laughter, but the utilization of your sense of humor will take some effort. And it is well worth the effort. We've all experienced situations when we said, "*One day we will look back on this and laugh.*" By cultivating your sense of humor you can gain some insight so that you can actually enjoy the humor when it happens.

1. *It starts with a smile.*

Don't underestimate the power of a smile. A smile is the gateway to laughter. Smiling is a means of communicating pleasure. Whether it comes from the memory of a story or the sight of a child—find a reason to smile. Smiling is the first defense against anger and frustration and it's the first indication of pleasure. You cannot enjoy laughter or humor without first making way for a smile.

2. *Learn the many resources of humor.*

Humor can be found in all areas of our life. In our home on the job or just walking down the street—recognize it and enjoy it. Refer to the quiz, "Could I have Humor in My Environment?,"

Learn how you view your humor and the resources that you have. After completing the questionnaire, ask yourself the following: *What did I learn about my humor? Am I a humor consumer and do I value my sense of humor? Can I improve on my utilization of humor?*

Always seek to improve your sense of humor and continue using it. After all, regular laughter reportedly adds eight years to our life. Everyone's sense of humor is unique and this uniqueness will determine how many humor resources we have.

Humor is also a reflection of our attitude and how we view life. Identify your personal humor resources and let them work for you. If you enjoy situational comedies, take time to watch your favorites. If you find the funnies give you a chuckle, then make sure to start your day with the comics. Learn your resources and begin using them regularly.

3. Schedule humor time.

Though humor can be found in all areas of our lives we still may need to schedule some time for laughter and wit. Identify your favorite comedians and find time to listen to their routines. Ask yourself what is it about these comedians that I like? How do you identify with their humor? Is it their view of life or something else? Whatever the reason try and find the time to enjoy it. Remember, you control your time so take a humor break daily.

A humor break will result in increased productivity and a more enjoyable life. One thing that never changes is there are 24 hours in a day and seven days in a week. Everyone's time is the same—from the President to the White House custodian—60 minutes in an hour and 24 four hours in every day. What we do with our time helps determine how we live. Schedule some time for humor and laughter.

4. Try new approaches to old routines.

We are all creatures of habit and many times our habits become routine. Try changing your routine. Brush your teeth with your opposite hand. Practice walking backwards with co-workers. Find a different route to work. Be creative and ask yourself if there is anything you can alter or do differently that can help make the day humorous. If you feel like you're in a rut, then grab a humor rope and pull yourself out. Trying new approaches to old routines may be the humor rope you need.

5. Share you humor.

Laughter is a wonderful gift and it needs to be shared. We should all find ways to share humor especially with our family and co-workers. Sharing laughter will not only improve our disposition but it can also affect the disposition of others. Laughter is a universal language and is understood by all. It may be shared by telling a joke, posting a funny sign or by sending a humorous email. Find ways to share your humor. As we begin to share our humor with others, they hopefully will in turn share it with you. Everyone should recognize the need to develop and share humor and the power it has on making a bad day good and good day better. Share and enjoy.

6. Exercise you humor.

Know what triggers your laughter. Recognize what makes you laugh and the keys to your humor. Review the "Humor Inventory". Become aware of what type of humor you enjoy and what makes you laugh and then find ways to increase it. Whether it is observational humor or jokes, find the source of your humor and exercise it. Once you have discovered what actually makes you laugh then cultivate it. Our humor needs to be exercised daily. Humor: use it or lose it.

7. Keep a humor file or joke jar.

When we have humor easily available it can brighten a dull or stressful day. Keep a resource of humor near your work area or in your home. When it is available you're more likely to exercise it. Collect cartoons from magazines and from the paper. Write down the jokes you enjoy and put them in a resource jar. If you found them humorous once they should be humorous again. Everyone can contribute to a humor file at work or in the home. Need a humor vacation? Pull something out of the joke jar. Keep the collection close and available. A humor collection can help you keep a proper perspective on the day's events.

Life begins at 40, but so do arthritis and the habit of telling the same story three times to the same person.

—Sam Levenson

8. Take a humor escape.

A five-minute humor escape is painless and inexpensive. The benefits of a humor escape affect us in all areas of our life—mentally, physically and socially. We've learned how a good dose of laughter positively effects our attitude as well as our outlook. So take a humor escape. The escape may be found in a humorous book, a cartoon or in the sharing of a joke. Find ways to celebrate your humor and strive to develop a routine that allows you to experience laughter regularly. Not only will you benefit but everyone you associate with will as well. Develop the discipline to seek laughter and to enjoy laughter. Always remember the importance of injecting humor into your attitude.

9. Develop a positive environment.

Our environment plays a major role in how we feel and how we interact with others. We should find ways to make our environment positive and, if possible, supportive. If laughter is part of our environment then we are ahead of the game. Surround yourself with positive friends and positive outlets. A positive attitude, like laughter, can be contagious. Try not to be brought down by the naysayers of life. Remember, a positive attitude can be enhanced by a positive environment. Create an environment for enjoyment and positive growth.

10. Have outlets for humor and enjoyment.

Keep a list of fun activities you enjoy that cost less than $10. Make a list of fairly inexpensive things you enjoy and then use it for you personal outlet. Maybe it's going to the movies, purchasing a funny book or a special snack. There are many inexpensive outlets for fun and humor. Your list should be a reflection of things that work for you and things you like to do. Make a list of people and things that bring pleasure and enjoyment to your life. An attitude adjustment may just be a laugh away; increase you resources.

11. Join the toy of the month club.

A little non-sensical fun can go a long way. Keep small toys available at your desk—windup toys, bubbles, a slinky and stress ball are all items that can provide a short break from the daily grind. Who knows, maybe the next time you are put on hold, the time may pass quicker by using one of these toys for a mental break. A variety of toys and humorous objects can help you keep your stress in check, while improving your attitude with a smile.

12. Seek humorous information from others.

The people you live with and work with constantly influence your use of humor. Ask the people you trust for their input about your humor. What do they think about your humor? Do they think you need to lighten up a bit? Ask for their impressions. The information can be very valuable as you develop a humor plan for work or home.

13. Rediscover the child within.

Everyone has an inner child waiting to play. Recount what you did as a child to have fun. What made you laugh? Who made you laugh? What was it about those childhood memories that were so much fun? Find the child within and begin enjoying him or her. Make a list of things that you really enjoyed. From this list begin finding ways to recapture the enjoyment and good feelings you experienced. Become a healthier adult by exercising the inner child.

14. Laugh at yourself.

Remember that life is too serious to take serious. Everyone makes mistakes and there are times we need to look at those mistakes with a humorous eye. The ability to laugh at ourselves takes self-confidence. Relax and find humor in some of your personal blunders. By doing this, you give yourself energy to move forward and not be trapped in a negative situation. Find ways to laugh at yourself; don't fear embarrassment—if you enjoy the humor in the moment others will as well. If we can't laugh at ourselves then who can we laugh at?

When you begin cultivating your sense of humor it is important to remember the vowels of humor

A Awareness

Be aware of the humor that surrounds you. Be aware of the many benefits of a good laugh.

I Involvement

Involve yourself in your humor. Share your humor with others and demonstrate the power of a good laugh.

O Open

Be open to the humor that you encounter daily. Be open to others and their humor and laughter and return the gift.

U Utilize

Utilize your sense of humor in the home, on the road and at work. Always allow for the utilization of humor.

E Enjoy

Enjoy the humor that surrounds you and give yourself permission to take time to laugh. There are few things more enjoyable and more important to a balanced life.

Y You

You make the difference. You decide whether to use your humor resource or not. You make the difference when it comes to how you use your sense of humor.

Chapter 11

See Funny, Hear Funny, Speak Funny
Developing Comic Vision

Comic vision, what is it and where can I find it? This may be the $64,000 question. I know that is an old reference, but it just sounds better than the million dollar question. A simple definition of comic vision would be: having the ability to recognize and enjoy the humor that surrounds us. Comic vision is a personal trait. It may not be as unique as our fingerprint but it is still up to the individual.

They say beauty is in the eye of the beholder. Well, so is comic vision. This makes it difficult to define. Many times friends will enjoy the same types of humor but when it is all said and done comic vision is up to the individual.

The hit TV show "Seinfeld" billed itself as a show about nothing. They took everyday events and created a successful show that millions could relate to. The success of the show was dependent on the writers being able to demonstrate comic vision. They presented everyday storylines that viewers could identify with in a humorous fashion. They were able to take everyday life and show its humor and, in doing so, created a successful comedy series.

Some of the most successful stand-up comedians use their comic vision to create a story or situations that the audience can relate to. The laughter arises from the listeners relating to the story. This is comic vision—the ability to see humor in normal occurrences. Of course, one's comic vision is dependent on one's attitude at the time. It also is dependent on how the world is viewed. Just as jokes depend on how an individual hears and internalizes the joke, comic vision is dependent on how we view life and what may be happening at the time.

If you are constantly feeling stress and feeling as if your mission in life is to put a square peg in a round hole then you will have trouble recognizing your comic vision. To develop our own comic vision we need to give ourselves permission to see and enjoy the humor that surrounds us. Too often our attitude will put up a road block preventing us from using our humor. When this happens, we may find ourselves suffering from a poor attitude or a stressful disposition. In chapter 5, I spoke about changing our view of traffic jams and how a simple "moo" could help change our perception and lower the stress of the moment. This is comic vision. We have to step back from the negative, start recognizing the humor and take control over our attitude.

How do I find comic vision?

You will need a little energy and may even need some practice. Like learning to tell jokes, you may need to give it some time. You can't learn comic vision over night, however the learning process should be fun and challenging.

One way of practicing comic vision is to begin looking at the world with a different frame of reference. The TV show "Candid Camera" caught thousands of people on camera experiencing the unexpected. They encountered situations that were not congruent to what they expected. Make yourself the cameraman and begin seeing the world differently. Maybe it is a water fountain mishap, or someone spilling a drink—just begin seeing the silly, goofy things people say and do and give yourself permission to laugh. When we begin taking a humorous view of the world we are using comic vision. Don't find humor in the misfortune of others, but find humor in the normal occurrences of life.

Defining and Discovering Comic Vision

Comic vision is the ability to see humor in our world. Maybe it is seeing the humor in an innocent road sign or in a newspaper headline. When you have a comic eye you will begin seeing humor in all kinds of places.

A humor break can be enjoyed when we use our comic vision. It may only last a few seconds, but a few seconds of laughter outweigh hours of stress.

"Sometimes I hear people say things they never said. Sometimes I see people do things they never did. I hope you do, too."

—Billy Crystal

Developing an eye for comic vision may take a little creative thinking and some silliness. The following exercises are designed to help you begin developing your comic vision. As with any humor exercise, it's supposed to be fun, not stressful. Take a few minutes to complete the exercises putting your creativity to work. Hopefully the end results will be improved comic vision and a new way to look at our world. Have fun.

Complete the following Humor Inventory work sheets to better understand your sense of humor and how you see the world and how the world sees you.

If they were to make a movie of your career it could be titled?

A. Dangerous Liaisons   B. Six Feet Under
C. The Terminator   C. Mad Mad Mad World
D. Other _____

How would you describe your work environment?

A. Happy Days   B. Jeopardy
C. Friends   C. I've got a Secret
D. Dark Shadows

How would you describe your sense of humor?

A. Survivor   B. Law and Order
C. Concentration   D. The Price is Right
E. Other _____

Friends would describe your sense of humor as?

A. Gone in Sixty Seconds B. Gone with the Wind
C. Happy Gilmore   D. Rawhide
E. Other _____

The best way to describe my joke telling ability is?

A. Fantasy Island   B. Lost
C. Mission Impossible   D. 60 Minutes
E. Other _____

6. If you were cast as an animated character who would it be?

A. Snow White   B. Goofy
C. Shrek   D. Dumbo
E. Other _____

7. My co-workers may cast me as:

A. Prince Charming   B. Wicked Witch
C. Buzz Light Year   D. Pollyanna
E. Other _____

8. What prevents you from telling jokes?

A. Bad timing   B. Can't remember jokes
C. Lack of confidence   D. Nothing
E. Other _____

9. Do you remember the last time you told a joke?

10. Do you remember the last time you made someone laugh?

11. Do you read the newspaper comics? If so how often?

12. Do you have a favorite comic strip or one you relate too?

13. Do you watch comedy on TV? If so, what are your favorites?

14. Do you have a favorite comedy movie that you will watch over and over?

15. Do you have favorite comedians? If so, who are they?
    a. What is it about their style humor that appeals to you?
    b. How do you relate to their humor?
    c. Who do you share this appreciation of humor with?

16. Do you consider yourself a humor consumer?
    a. If so, what are your humor outlets?
    b. How do you use your humor?

Creativity is a large part of comic vision. Being creative with your vision and being creative with your thinking. The more you practice your comic vision the more you will benefit from it. The following exercise is designed to help us tap into our creative thinking.

Complete the following "EXAGGERABLES"

Mama said there would be days like this but she never said _____

To think I chose this job for

_____

My job is so boring that

_____

I am so busy at work that you would think

_____

I'm not saying the boss is dumb but if you were to ask him the meaning of life he would tell you

_____

One day I am going to walk into work and

_____

At the office we found that it only takes

_____**to**

change a _____

The most excitement we have had was when the

_____

Rough? Talk about rough! My job was so rough that

_____

Complete the following "DRUTHERS."

I would rather spend an hour with an angry skunk than

_____

I would rather drink a gallon of beach water than

_____

I would rather take a shower with kerosene than go

_____

I would rather eat sea weed than

_____

**I'd rather watch the national spelling
bee for 48 hours straight than**

_____

_____

Sometimes it comes down to how creative we think. A little creative thinking can go a long way in our humor development. True comic vision is being able to see humor in the mundane. Too often we allow our schedules to dictate what type of attitude we have. We end up missing out on many opportunities for laugher and fun. If this is happening to you it may be time to slow down and begin putting your comic vision to work.

Remember that comic vision is in the eye of the beholder. What I see as being funny you may not and vice versa. What is important is that we recognize our own comic vision and then put it to work.

Putting Comic Vision to Work

The following sections of the book are dedicated to finding humor in the way we live and see things differently.

Over Twenty Five
Things to Consider around the Copy Machine

Do married people live longer or does it just seem that way?

You ever notice that when you dial a wrong number you never get a busy signal?

Everything is within walking distance if you have the time.

What do batteries run on?

It doesn't matter what temperature a room is, it is always room temperature.

After they make Styrofoam what do they ship it in?

How young can you die of old age?

If you were going to arrest a mime would you have to tell him he has the right to remain silent?

If you were going to shoot a mime would you have to use a silencer?

If your personal vehicle was a UPS truck could you park anywhere?

What is another word for thesaurus?

Is a turtle with no shell naked or homeless?

If toast always lands butter side down and a cat always lands on his feet, what happens if you strap a piece of toast on the cat and drop it?

If you are cross-eyed and dyslexic, can you read ok?

Why did the castaways have so many clothes? It was a three-hour tour.

If you were to have a funeral at night would you turn off your lights?

Why do we open our months when we listen intently?

Why is it that when we are lost and looking for an address the first thing we do is turn down the radio?

Why do stores that are open 24 hours have locks?

What does Geronimo say when he jumps from a plane?

Can someone die in a living room?

Do vegetarians eat animal crackers?

Why does sour cream have an expiration date?

Why did kamikaze pilots wear helmets?

When a cow laughs does milk come out its nose?

Why is rush hour traffic so slow?

Do hermits have peer pressure?

Why is lemon juice made form artificial flavoring and floor wax from real lemons?

Do we get distressed leather from stressed out cows?

The roadways are full of humor. It may be in a sign on the highway or on a bumper sticker of a passing car. Bumper stickers and signs can say one thing and be interpreted in a different way. All it takes to see things differently is a little comic vision. There are plenty of resources for humor that can be enjoyed. The following signs have brightened up my days and I hope they do the same for you.

Signs Along the Way

```
Do Not

Mow

Test Plot
```

I see this sign almost every time I travel on an interstate. Is this a problem? Never have I said to my wife, I think I will crank up the mower and go down to the interstate and mow awhile. Personally I feel people have enough to worry about without having to take time to mow the interstate highways. But obviously it is a problem or why else would we have so many signs telling us not to mow? I will say this about this sign: it is one of power. Think about it. You put up this sign in your front yard and you would never have to mow. The neighbors couldn't say a thing you can't cut your grass—your yard is a test plot. I may need to get me one these signs.

Some signs just worry me. One is a sign at a local cemetery that gives these instructions.

Parking For
Customers
Only

I don't know about you but I am in no hurry to be a customer. I'm not parking there.

A local fast food chain put up the following sign; maybe you will see the humor in it.

Coming Soon Fried Chicken
Applications Being Accepted

I could just see the chickens lining up to apply for this once in a lifetime and I do mean once in a lifetime opportunity.

Sometimes you can see the humor in what people are trying to sell. This sign appeared in my neighborhood.

For Sale
Live Puppies

I did so want to stop and look over these puppies and say, "Why these puppies are all alive!"

We had a drycleaner that had this sign up for eight weeks. One could only assume they were having a SHIRT Special

SHI T SPECIAL .99

My curiosity finally got to me and I ventured inside only to see another sign stating:

Drop Pants Here

I ran from the store.
In a small town in South Carolina I saw this sign,

Urgent Care
Same Day Service
No Appointment Necessary

When in need of urgent care it usually is on the same day and generally speaking you may not have an appointment. I just imagine someone breaking their arm, and then calling for an appointment and getting it for the next week. Not at this urgent care center you can be seen on the same day with no appointment.

At a truck stop: **Eat Here**
Get Gas

I like to call this one truth in advertising.

Ears Pierced
While you wait This sign appeared in a local jewelry store. In all honesty I didn't know you had a choice. I never notice anyone drop off their ears for piercing.

All Baggage This sign at local airport make one
Carts Must wonder if this is a problem. I know
Yield luggage is being made better but to
Right Away take on an airplane. No, thank you.
To Oncoming
Aircraft

This sign appeared on the road to a local beach. **Warning**
I'm really not sure our tax dollars are being used **Road Wet**
wisely when we need a sign of this nature. **When**
Maybe the money should go into education. **Raining**
The Johnson Clinic

This is truly a marketing genius think of it **Veterinarian**
either way you get your dog back. **Taxidermist**

A local church had the following invitation for passersby:

Sunday May 24

Come in and hear
what Hell is really like.

Choir sings at every service.

Obviously the choir director had little say in this message. Sometimes you can see the humor in the way people advertise there services.

On a plumber's truck:

A Straight Flush
Beats a Full House

At a Radiator repair shop:

Best Place to
Take a Leak

On an Electrician's truck:

Give Us
Your Shorts

At a local funeral home:

Ask About Our
Lay Away Plans

On your next trip begin looking for humor on the highway. Hopefully you will see some humor and enjoy your trip more.

It's a funny world enjoy it

Another way of developing comic vision is to begin collecting things that you may think are funny. To paraphrase Steven Wright, "It is a funny world we live in but I wouldn't want to paint it." If you see a headline in the paper and it makes you laugh, cut it out or write it down to share with others. This may require a little discipline on your part, but it will be well worth your efforts. Sometimes we see the humor maybe thinking, 'now that's funny,' but we never think of it again. Discipline yourself to take time and collect humor and you will appreciate it later. Keep a joke journal. Begin collecting items you come across that make you laugh. Then, if you are having one of those days all you will really need do is pull out your humor collection and begin smiling.

Make your own comic resource. My humor resource is a notebook I keep with me containing various collections of things that I found humor in. I often share this humor with others in my presentations or in workshops. I will also share it with friends who are in need of a humor vacation.

Bumper Stickers I wish I had seen or have seen:

I intend to live forever—so far, so good.

When everything is coming your way,

you're in the wrong lane.

Do you follow this close at work?

If you don't like my driving stay off the sidewalk.

Everyone has bad days; the following list would indicate some days are worse than others and maybe you should have stayed in bed. You know it is going to be a bad day when ....

Your blind date turns out to be your ex-wife.

The bird singing outside your window is a vulture.

Your birthday cake collapses from the weight of the candles.

The candles on your birthday cake set off the smoke detector.

Your income tax refund check bounces.

Your twin forgets your birthday.

A *60 Minutes* crew is waiting outside your office.

Suicide prevention puts you on hold.

You call 911 and they ask if you could call back at a later time.

Another collection I have is of actual insurance claims. When asked to write down a brief statement of the accident this is how some replied.

A pedestrian hit me and went under my car.

I pulled away from the side of the road, glanced at my mother in law and headed over the embankment.

The accident occurred when I was attempting to bring my car out of a skid by steering it into the other vehicle.

My car was legally parked when I backed into the pedestrian.

An invisible car came out of nowhere, struck my vehicle and vanished.

In an attempt to kill a fly I drove into a telephone poll.

The telephone poll was approaching fast; I was attempting to swerve out of its way when it struck the front of my car.

The other car crashed into my car without giving any warning of his intention.

The guy was all over the road I had to swerve a number of times before I finally hit him.

When I saw I could not avoid a collision, I stepped on the gas and crashed into the other car.

Church Bulletins can be a good source of humor. Just look at this list of actual slips that appeared in church bulletins across the country.

Wednesday the Ladies Literary Society will meet and Mrs. Lacey will sing "Put me in my Little Bed" accompanied by the Reverend.

This afternoon there will be a meeting in the north and south ends of

the church and children will be baptized at both ends.

Don't let worry kill you. Let the church help

Remember in prayer the many that are sick of our church and community.

Tuesday at 7:00 pm there will be an ice cream social. All ladies giving milk please come early.

This Sunday being Easter we will invite Mrs. Jones to come forward and lay an egg on the altar.

A source of humor that all parents have probably contributed to is in the excuses written for our children after they have missed school. When your child misses school it is up to the parent to write a note explaining the absence. If your children are anything like mine they remind you to write the excuse as they are putting one foot on the bus. You quickly grab a piece of paper and hurriedly scribble something down. As you watch your child's bus pull out you begin wondering 'What did I write?" The following collection is of actual excuses given to teachers.

Jerry has been absent he had two teeth taken out of his face.

Please excuse Johnny for being absent on January 28, 29, 30, 31, and 32. He had an acre on his side.

My son is under doctor's care and should not take PE. Please execute him.

Marion was sick. She was in bed under the doctor and

could not get up.

Please excuse Mary from being absent. She was sick and I had her shot.

Please excuse my daughter's absence from school. She had a bad case of the fool last week.

So the next time you are called on to write an excuse remember you may be supplying a little needed humor to a teacher. With any luck your excuse can appear in a book.

Sometimes the humor is no further than your newspaper. Many a funny headline has given people the opportunity to laugh or ask, "Was that what they wanted to say?" Here are some examples from my local newspaper that I have collected over the years.

Local Cemetery Praised By Former Residents

Man Holds Himself Hostage for Seven Hours

Aging Director Hired

Mall Merchants Settle with Hooker

Exhibitionist Show More Stuff

Death Ends Fun

Governor Ask Support for Waste Ban

Workers Contain Gas

Funeral Ends in Death

Boys Cause as Many Pregnancy's as Girls

Furniture Drive for Homeless Announced

Trees can Break Wind

Living Together Link to Divorce

You may find the humor in the comic section but as seen from these examples you may also find it unexpectedly in the headlines.

Every day presents a new opportunity to find humor. If we are open to humor we will surely begin seeing it. Sometimes humor presents itself in some unlikely places; just be receptive to it. The old saying, 'Slow down and smell the roses,' can be changed slightly to 'Slow down and enjoy the laughter.'

Chapter 12

That's All Folks

George Carlin once said, "People who go through life and fail to see its humor are missing the point." I agree whole heartily with Carlin and would like to add to the statement. If you go through life and fail to see its humor you may not only be missing the point, but could also be missing out on an opportunity for joy, relaxation, contentment, a positive attitude and so on and so on. Joy is not an event it's a journey and the road to joy can be paved with humor.

Hopefully the information contained in this book can help you on your journey in life. Humor is essential for a balanced life. William Frye M.D. a professor of psychiatry at Stanford University Medical School has studied humor for years and he has found that the average kindergartner laughs around 300 times a day and the average adult only 17. When the rate of laughter was addressed in previous chapters it was easy to see that stress and anxiety take their toll on adults and as we age we become more uptight. If we find ourselves uptight and stressed, laughter will not occur and if you don't have an outlet for laughter you may be losing the battle for a balanced life. It's simple—we all have the need for humor and laughter and when it is present life is better. Humor is everywhere. It's a universal language that can be understood and enjoyed by everyone.

We should all try to cultivate our sense of humor. There shouldn't be a need for a book titled *Better Living through Laughter*, but, unfortunately, far too many of us find ourselves in need of a refresher course on laughter. My effort to put my workshop ideas and my thoughts of humor down on paper is more a celebration of laughter and fun, and how it has served me. A better life can be realized when we allow for humor. We should seek out humor and enjoy a good laugh. It's easy to neglect humor or fail to use our sense of humor and, like anything else in life, if we fail to use it we will lose it. A good rule for our sense of humor would be: don't lose it, use it.

If we are open to humor we will see everyday situations that promote laughter. But if we are not open to it, it may as well be a lottery ticket that goes unclaimed. By allowing ourselves to recognize humor we are creating a means for enjoyment. And with enjoyment we also begin to actualize the many benefits of laughter. We will see our mental and physical health improve with each laugh. Such is the power of laughter. Never underestimate the value of laughter and a good sense of humor.

If we are free to enjoy humorous events and we take time to share laughter we are freeing up our attitude for positive growth. When we allow for this freedom of expression and enjoyment we will be less likely to put restraints on it. Too many of us put conditions on our happiness. You know the type of person who qualifies their happiness. They put restrictions on being happy. We have all heard them with the statement, "I'll be happy when…" They have the attitude that happiness is tied to an event and will come later. They find themselves preoccupied with other events, thus preventing them from enjoying the immediacy of happiness. Try not to be the one who says, "I will be happy when…" Here are some examples of how people put the brakes on happiness:

As soon as I get that promotion I can be happy.

Man, once I lose that weight I am going to be so happy.

I'll be happy when the kids are off to college.

When I get that car I will be one happy guy.

When we get this project complete we can then be happy.

I'll be happy when I retire.

Don't misunderstand me—I'm not saying these events shouldn't make you happy but don't let the event be the determining factor in your happiness. If you find yourself putting conditions on your happiness, you will never truly be happy. The promotion may come, but with it comes greater stress; the new car may have it all but it may also come with a new payment plan. You name it and conditional happiness will produce more conditions and you end up cheating yourself out of many an opportunity for enjoyment. Resist putting conditions on your happiness. Without conditions, happiness may knock on our door with conditions we may never hear the knock.

A friend of mine once told me a story of his grandmother, Amy Tisdale, who on her 100th birthday was asked if there was anything she would have done differently. After several seconds of contemplation, with a sly smile she replied, "I would have eaten the doughnut." She would have eaten the doughnut! Think about that statement. If we allow ourselves to enjoy the moment we will be less likely to have regrets later in life.

There are many doughnuts in life and laughter is just one of them. Don't find yourself being asked what you would have done differently and your answer being, "laugh more." Laughter is free and abundant. It just takes us allowing for its enjoyment. No restrictions. No time tables. Enjoy it when you find it.

I feel fortunate that I discovered early on that a good laugh beats a stressful day anytime. As I mentioned in the stress management chapter stress is alive and well but an antidote to stress may be as simple as putting a humorous perspective on it. We are faced with life's challenges continually and our humor is a tool that can help us deal with negative and positive situations alike. A dose of humor and a good laugh all contribute to an improved attitude and positive outlook. The benefits of laughter are many—no matter where you go or what you do. Life is a journey and our humor should be considered a road map for the journey.

We can only reap the benefits of a good laugh or a funny situation when we allow them to take place. I realize this sounds fairly simple, but in reality it can be a difficult challenge—but the challenge is well worth the effort. Become serious about your humor; practice it and use it regularly. Hopefully you can incorporate some of the ideas presented in this book into your life and how you approach it. Look back over the humor inventory and learn something about your humor and how you use it. Can it be improved? Only you can answer the question. Practice your humor with loved ones, friends and co-workers and soon you will discover that everyone benefits from sharing a smile or a laugh.

Maybe you have used some of the exercises ideas presented in the past. Hopefully you see the value of humor and how it can improve or enrich your life in the home, at work or wherever you find yourself. Always pack your sense of humor. Remember, laughter is a gift that keeps on giving. Give and accept the gift of laughter. A smile is contagious and a laugh is infectious. Share whenever possible.

Okay that wasn't all, but this is!

I never dreamed when I started this project how long it would take me to actually finish. But I did finish and for that I am grateful. I have learned some valuable lessons on this journey. The hardest lesson was learning that writing a book about humor is much more difficult than speaking about humor. Whenever I have been asked to speak to groups or organization it has come easy to me. But when it came to writing down my thoughts on humor I experienced a whole new level of anxiety and stress. For years I have done workshops and presentations concerning humor and laughter. Sharing a laugh is personal and gratifying. But the experience of putting my thoughts down on paper was an entirely different animal to me. When it was all said and done, the project took close to five years to finish and in that time I have had some unexpected highs and few unexpected lows.

My finished product differs greatly from the original draft. And believe me that is a good thing, but the focus of the book has always remained the same. Celebrate humor and share the premise that one can have a better life if we allow for laughter.

Since those beginning days, I have experienced a lot of change in my life. From work to my personal life, it seems the only constant has been that of change. Zachary and Andrew have both graduated from college and are living their own version of better living through laughter. They continue to call with jokes and funny antidotes. Whenever we get together you can bet laughter is present. I cherish the laughter we share and I feel it is a legacy I have passed on to them. They both grasp and celebrate the idea that laughter is as valuable at work as it is in the home. Lila who helped with many of the drawings in the book is growing up so fast and she is enjoying the life of the much younger sibling. She finds it humorous that her dad is sometimes confused for her grandfather. Such is the life of an aging parent. Drew has developed into quite a young man. He still has many challenges and battles ahead but you can bet he will always bring on a smile and a chuckle when you see him.

Many things have taken place in the last five years. Our country has had its share of ups and downs. From fighting two wars to fighting a slumping economy, we have had plenty of reasons to feel down. But this is when our sense of humor is needed most. If we can find some humor in our challenges we can begin to accept our challenges. With acceptance comes the ability to deal with the challenge and acceptance can be realized through a good laugh.

I am sad to say that I lost my dear mother during the writing of this book I use the term lost rather than died because that is how I feel. With her death, I felt as I had lost not only a wonderful mother but also an inspiration for the use of humor and the enjoyment of laughter. I chose not to make any adjustments to the text as a tribute to her and the way she lived. Her humor lives on daily as I speak with my brother and talk with those who knew her and loved her laughter is always present.

As I put down my thoughts on humor and shared ideas and stories I always felt my mother's spirit and support. That is the strength of a shared smile and a good laugh. The results stay with us long after the smile has dissipated and the laughter has stopped. I know my mother would have loved this book she may have been the only one, but she would have loved it. That was the power of her attitude.

Up until the end Mom continued to smile and her infectious laughter was always present. Her positive outlook on life and her sense of humor was a gift everyone who knew and loved her enjoyed.

Barry and I have spoken of how Mom's laughter in many ways was like the hugs she gave us as children. They both made us feel warm and comfortable. She had a simple philosophy that served her well for 82 years: "Smile, laugh and enjoy life." Every day I miss my mother I wish I could simply get in the car and go for a visit or pick up the phone and give her a call.

Unfortunately those days are gone, but I have her memory and the memories of my father as well. My parents taught me a great deal about life but the life lesson I cherish the most is to value and appreciate laughter. Don't hesitate to share a laugh or a smile. Life is tough enough with laughter; don't make it any tougher by not enjoying the fruits of laughter and humor. In many ways the person I am today was forged by my parents and how they chose to share laughter. Everyday no matter what the circumstance you could always count on some laughter.

I continue to seek out laughter when possible. I have learned the value of a smile and a little chuckle and how both can open doors to opportunities as well as disarm our enemies. Laughter affects the way we live and the enjoyment we find in life. If we are smiling and laughing we are better equipped for the daily challenges no matter what they are. Plato once said, "Even the gods love jokes. I'm not sure what gods he was referring to but I feel he was telling us that by sharing humor we can find peace with our self and with others. The Koran says, "A man deserves paradise that makes his companions laugh." I would like to take some editorial licenses on this statement and change it to read, "He who makes his companions laugh will enjoy paradise on earth." In many ways this is how I remember my mother. Mom always found paradise no matter where life took her. The paradise she enjoyed was directly related to how she used her sense of humor and the way she found humor in everything around her. She never hesitated to laugh at herself or enjoy a shared laugh with others.

I still take time to listen to my favorite comedians and that list continues to grow. Today, there are so many outlets for all types of humor so many in fact that no one should have an excuse for not enjoying a laugh. But regrettably too many people still refuse to allow humor into their lives. Don't be one of those individuals. Rediscover your own resources for humor and put them to work. It's important to remember that laughter can dissolve tension and anxiety and it gives us a resource when we have to deal with grief or anger. Laughter is an emotional release and as with any emotional release, a cleansing affect can take place. When laughter supplies the release, a cleansing of your attitude can take place. You will feel the benefits of laughter both physically and emotionally and in the process you will also strengthen your character and improve your disposition.

Go ahead make my day. Laugh...

Bibliography

A Time to Laugh , *The Religion of Humor,* Donald Capps Continuum Press, New York, New York 2005

Adaptation to Life, George Valliant Harvard University Press, Boston Mass. 1976

Anatomy of an Illness, Norman Cousins Bantam Press, Boston Mass. 1976

Braude's Treasury of Wit and Humor, Joseph Braude Prentice Hall Inc. Englewood California, 1964

Humor Works, John Morreall Ph.D. HRD Press, Amherst MA. 1997

How to be Funny, Steve Allen and Jane Wollman McGraw Hill Book Company NY, NY 1987

Laughing Matters, *A Celebration of American Humor* Gene Shalit Ballantine Books NY, NY

The Craft of Comedy Writing Sol Saks Writers Digest Books Cincinnati Ohio 1985

The Healing Power of Humor, Allen Klien J.P. Tancher Inc. Los Angeles, CA. 1989

You Gatta Keep Dancin Tim Hansel Guidepost Caramel NY, 1985

1,000 One Liners Henny Youngman Ballymote Books Kantanal NY 1989